THE SISTERS
ANTIPODES

Also by JANE ALISON

The Love-Artist

The Marriage of the Sea

Natives and Exotics

JANE ALISON

THE SISTERS
ANTIPODES

HOUGHTON MIFFLIN HARCOURT

BOSTON · NEW YORK

2009

For information about permission to reproduce selections from this book,
write to Permissions, Houghton Mifflin Harcourt Publishing Company,
6277 Sea Harbor Drive, Orlando, Florida 32887-6777.

www.hmhbooks.com

Library of Congress Cataloging-in-Publication Data
Alison, Jane.
Sisters antipodes/Jane Alison. — 1st ed.
p.   cm.
ISBN 978-0-15-101280-0
1. Alison, Jane — Family.   2. Alison, Jane — Childhood and youth.
3. Novelists, American — 21st century — Biography.   I. Title.
PS3551.L366Z475   2009
813'.54 — dc22   [B]   2008014747

Text set in ITC Legacy Serif
Designed by Linda Lockowitz

Printed in the United States of America

DOC 10 9 8 7 6 5 4 3 2 1

THE SISTERS
ANTIPODES

In 1965, when I was four, my parents met another couple, got along well, and within a few months traded partners. This was in Canberra, where my father, an Australian diplomat, had just brought us home from a posting in Washington. The other couple were American but diplomats, too, finishing a post in Canberra before returning to the United States. Both men were in their early thirties, tall, slim, and ambitious; both women were smart and good-looking. Both couples had two little girls the same ages, and the younger girls shared a birthday and almost the same name. This was my counterpart, Jenny, and me. The two families had so much in common, people said: They must meet.

The couples fascinated each other at once, I am told, and for the next months we were together constantly for picnics, outings, dinners. My father's and Paul's cars raced from Canberra, and we'd park in glades of eucalypts and spread out big plaid blankets. After lunch my sister and I and the other two girls would be sent to play, to find a koala or kangaroo, and we'd wander into the heat and buzzing stillness with sticks, hitting peeled trunks, prodding for snakes, as our parents murmured and laughed and lounged on blankets and clinked their beers or glasses of wine.

Later, I'd be put in a bath with Jenny. We had the same birthday, but she was a year older, and we looked alike enough to be sisters — little girls with wavy hair and bright staring eyes, although mine were blue and hers were brown. I see us in the bath gazing at each other over sudsy water, our wrinkled pink feet pressed together and pushing, as music and smoke drift under the door. We don't know that soon she'll live with my father and I'll live with hers, that for seven years we'll shadow each other around the globe, that the split will form everything about us: that we will grow up as each other's antipode.

The literal meaning of *antipodes*: two bodies pressed together, foot to foot.

In less than a year it was done. My mother, sister, and I would follow Paul to Washington, and my father would soon resume his diplomatic path with Helen and her girls: like continents splitting and sliding apart, each with its own living creatures. Pictures show the last hours Maggy and I spent with our father. The three of us pose by Lake Burley Griffin, where he kneels like a suitor and clasps one of us in each arm, earnest hope straining his thin face, while I cover my mouth and giggle. Then we left and flew to Washington. We didn't see or speak to him for seven years. Letters traveled over the oceans.

In 1973, we all landed on the same continent for the first time since the split. We were back in Washington, and the other family had been posted to New York, so Maggy and I could take the Amtrak north to see our father, and Patricia and Jenny could take it south to see theirs. Most often we went to my father's Upper East Side apartment when the girls were there. Jenny and I slept in twin beds in her pink room; Maggy and Patricia, in her yellow room beside us. Daddy and Helen slept at the other end of the apartment in the master bedroom, which was silken and civilized and looked over Fifth Avenue with its leashed poodles and gated trees. Between that master bedroom and us ran a very long, narrow carpeted hallway through which you could pace silently, stealthy. Photos show its wallpaper patterned like a garden trellis, but I remember it as bamboo, a jungle, and am sure that outside the photos' frames the wallpaper twines and transforms.

One of the first nights at our deep end of the hall, Jenny and I lay side by side in the dark, hot after handstands and wrestling. Her window opened onto a sooty space between buildings, and faint sounds of cars and distant voices floated in, her radio playing between us. She was twelve, I was eleven.

When you were young and your heart was an open book . . .

She sighed and stretched her arms, lifted a leg free of the sheets, and pointed her toes into the darkness. Then she turned to me and whispered, "So, who do you think did it first?"

Because this was the point. The split could not have been simultaneous and fair; things like that can't happen. One of our fathers had been ready to leave his own girls if he had to, and the other must have had less choice. One of our mothers had chosen a new man and won him, and the other woman must have lost. And whoever had won, whoever had lost, whoever had been easily left: That would determine who Jenny and I were, what each of us was worth.

1

Sometimes I think we all have embedded in the brain a personal place like a home we've lost that lingers in our skulls, and a pantheon of people who so imprinted us when we were young that we see everyone after in contrast. This place and these people — they're like elements or primary colors, forming and haunting our lives. *She* was the original green, and this woman is like her but a touch more blue. *He* was first red, and this man is like him, but darker.

The original place I've lost is Australia. A gum's peeling bark, a kangaroo's tail as it belts into the trees, the screams of a kookaburra hacking the air — the original place isn't ideal, just primary, saturating your child sensibility like the first exposure of film; if that place is then lost it settles in the brain rare and fantastic. Australia inspires fantasy, anyway, the great southern continent having been imagined and sought by Europe for so long, and this one so weird when found. From miles out at sea as English ships drew near, I have read, even over the pounding Pacific surf the racket of birds in this new world was incredible. I wish I could hear it and see it as early sailors did, squinting dazed across the foam: a riot of birds, untouched and shrieking, so innocent they could be hit with a stone. Lorikeets, white cockatoos, galahs, rosellas; and in the waters, enormous oysters, mussels, cockles, giant stingrays to be seized. So much that was unknowing and, to Europe, unknown: *Terra Nullius.*

The animals and plants resisted categories: Marsupials, which don't lay eggs or give birth to live young but release occult fetuses into daylight. The platypus, a mammal that lays eggs and lives in water. Flying squirrels. Trees that shed not leaves but bark, can be swallowed in flames, but spring up green from charred stumps. Captain James Cook and Joseph Banks and the others moved through this new world like Shakespeare's Miranda, although unlike her they sought possibilities, reasons to poke in a flag and lay claim. In New Zealand and Australia they gathered specimens: a small kangaroo they stuffed and mounted; flowers that looked like feathers or barnacles that they dried and dubbed names like *Banksia*; the skull of a Maori. After carving their ship's name on a eucalypt, they sailed back to the other side of the world, and two decades later British fleets returned with convicts, sheep, saplings, and seeds.

The Australia bobbing in my skull when I flew away at four is almost the one Cook and Banks saw. Climbing, squatting, poking, tasting, as a child you're close to the ground and all that wriggles on it, you can feel sensibility breathing everywhere, feel akin to small things: a gumnut, an echidna trembling in the grass. I still feel in my palm the papery bark of the eucalypt in front of our house, and how it peeled away, and the fairy gardens Maggy and I made, lying dreamy on our stomachs, arranging feathers and bottlebrush blossoms in the twisting roots of trees. And I see the garden made by our grandparents: Slight and white-maned in a cardigan, my grandfather Albert tends a philodendron as Maggy and I wander in nightgowns along pebble paths, among spiked palms, yellow wattle, blue gums. A place that came into being with each step you took through the shadows and sunlight, a place dangerously like paradise before we even knew the word.

When we flew away in 1966, we clutched things we'd been given to remember home: a stuffed kangaroo and koala, boomerangs, ink drawings of Aboriginal girls — the same things Cook and Banks took. We had books, too, so we wouldn't forget, the watercolor pictures conjuring a landscape of banksias and kookaburras as animate as Arcadia. I didn't go back to Australia for twenty years, and that country seemed to disappear from the world and slip into my head. But the place pulled as strongly as the mythical southern continent once had pulled those Englishmen two centuries earlier.

As for the pantheon: Maybe parents, brothers, sisters, are always the primary figures painted on your brain. The first examples of character — beauty or primness or a black comic bent — they swell into archetype before your eyes, become the hues and tissue from which you'll be made or through which you'll see others. My mother and Helen, my father and Paul, my sister and Patricia; Jenny. It wasn't just their colorings that lit them inside my skull but their doublings. A bicameral group to match the bihemisphered world we traveled after the split, and the bilateral brain and bichambered heart that slowly grew inside.

———

How it was before the split, how the split actually happened: There are a few simple facts, photos, and the shards I remember, but mostly the fragments of stories my four parents have told. Some of what's given as fact is plain, but not all, and pictures are partial. The pieces of memory from when you're four are like spots on a dirty window rubbed clear enough for light, color, an image to show through. You can rub these places, hoping to see more in the murk, *willing* that lost time to reappear, but it won't. And you can listen to the stories, sift them for truth, but one thing I know is that for my four parents, the truths are not the same.

My mother has told me the oldest fragments, pieces of the story I was too young to remember. Although I look for cracks in what she's said to find traces of different stories the others would tell, I know that I can't peel her words from my vision. Still, what she's told me is more tinged with wistfulness or rue than with the dark poison I think the others fear.

My father and mother grew up in South Australia in families that had been settled there just a few generations. The first had sailed from the British Isles and Nova Scotia in the 1800s: a gold miner, a shearer, an apothecary, a grocer. No convicts: These people came to the new world as pioneers. I don't want to know about the earlier generations. When the lines are traced back to England or Scotland, the pursuit becomes dark, muddy, heavy with clouds. Instead I see those settlers stepping onto Australia's shores like the first men and women stepping into the sun, and life and light begin.

I try to imagine those Anglo and Celtic settlers in Australia. How sharply etched they must have felt, their pale bodies standing alien against the alien landscape, casting different shadows in the new light, their thin pinkish skins stretched between their selves and the blistering sun. And what made those "selves": a language coursing in the blood; their names and the knowledge of where they'd come from; the ideas they'd brought of how things were done, how clothes were worn or a house was made or what green things should be pulled from the land, a land not yet packed with ancestral bones so all the more alien; a way of regarding through squinting eyes that would have to grow fierce in sheer opposition to all that lay threatening beyond, the self in its skin being so slight.

They struggled with the ground at their feet, prying up stones, ringbarking trees. A great-great uncle named Tom, a bushman, slept in mud in the rain and stood waist deep in a stream from morning to night helping sheep through the water. A great-grandfather Richmond arrived in Glenelg as the town was just forming and wrote dry letters about the state of the sidewalks. These first comers were literate, resourceful. One wrote letters aboard the *Clifton* as he crossed the Atlantic and Indian oceans, another published letters in the local paper, others wrote memoirs that glow with pride at each step closer to an anglicised world in the bush. A generation later, both my grandfathers were headmasters who looked out keenly as the place rose around them, annotating its progress. A great-aunt built her house from mallee roots and pulverized limestone and reported how grand was the day when a road came, then plumbing, and then electricity. The importance of the house, of making themselves *home*: My mother's mother, Dora, practiced shrewd domestic arts, reusing rinse water from the white laundry for the colors, keeping a cloth wet on the safe to chill milk. Whatever else their endeavor meant, these people transformed the foreign place to known, managed to make themselves home in it. My parents were the first to leave this new place, to look for something newer.

I have just five photographs of my parents together, along with a box of slides from the years of their marriage and a few pictures my father took of my mother while courting. The two met at university, and my father's first photos of my mother reveal both how she looked and how he must have looked at her, and to me this is the magic current: the current that invests what is seen with value. She stands laughing on a wide, bare beach at the bottom of Australia, the sand white and the water cold blue, her bare legs shapely and slender and her most beautiful feature, together with her sparkling eyes. She played tennis and field hockey and golf; on my desk I have a round silver box she won in a putting contest and a silver pencil cup as runner-up. Her nose is strong and Mediterranean, although there's no such blood in our line, and her mouth can seem either bawdy and wide or a small prim plum; herein lie her trickiness and potential. In photos of my mother and father they do not look well suited. In a newspaper picture at a party, his face seems alarmingly young and long, while beside him her eyes are lidded in a Cleopatra smile that seems knowing, although I doubt she knew much, was just restless and wanting to *go*, not sit potted at home. My father might have been restless, too — why else the diplomatic service? — but has always seemed concerned about propriety, how things are done. In the university library one evening, as the two were slipping on their jackets to leave, my mother tells me, she saw that her gloves were dirty. She leaned toward him over the table and whispered, What'll it be? Dirty gloves or no gloves?

He considered a moment and said, Dirty gloves.

Courting, he gave her a silver brush and mirror and a pair of sunglasses with tiny shutters like jalousies instead of tinted lenses. I would love to have those, to see what you saw through them, what sort of shuttered world you could make. My father is color blind. His mother, Maisie, became truly blind and wore a glass eye; my mother's father, Herbert, was deaf. My sister has one blue eye, one green eye. My mother has webbing between several toes.

In college my father and mother were called, she tells me, the Gruesome Twosome. Both have always had a weakness for puns.

In the wedding pictures taken outside the Anglican church, a pert white flower sits in my father's lapel, his hair is neatly combed back, and he grins like an excited schoolboy. White satin cuts my mother into voluptuous triangles, a cap sprays a pale shower of veil, and her sidelong smile is dangerous. They sailed for his first posting soon after. On deck in the blazing sun, she waves at the place she's abandoning, the new world their forebears had only just begun making, while he clasps her by the green-silk waist as if she needs anchoring already.

Then my mother dances the cancan at the British Cricket Club, flings her skirts above her head, but otherwise works to be a diplomat's wife. She makes curries and scones, cuts her own dresses from batik prints, haplessly freezes lettuce for a tropical picnic, gives birth to Maggy, and wears a white angel collar as she cradles her baby, her mouth the prim little plum. Then the young family moves to Canberra, home base, and I am born. Canberra was still fairly young for a city, and our house was a small bungalow in the hills, in a neighborhood being carved from the scrub, the trees and rocks around it ancient. I have one picture of my father holding me: A shadow falls upon his tilted face, and behind him spread the thin leaves of a bottlebrush or banksia. It's 1962.

At this point we move to Washington, and although my mother teaches, as she'd always do, something about her in the pictures grows wild. She's not suited for the diplomatic service, it seems; she's not happy. Her hair becomes tousled, and her expression, even her skin, seems darker. She wears sleeveless shifts that show her long limbs gleaming. As her hair grows, she looks less a neat concoction of the 1950s, more a reckless girl.

In 1965, she suns in the garden in a green bikini with her head thrown back and the book she's propped against her legs forgotten. I see my father pause at the window of our brick house and spy her — her legs liquid, face all light, troubling unsatisfied mouth sealed shut — and need to take this picture. The image appears in a sequence that begins with her as a slight figure in the green, then moves closer, snap by snap, until we stand above her as she sleeps, or thinks, or longs, or despairs, her eyes shut to the world and the sun. My father took many pictures in June and July 1965. Because she was beautiful and he wished to record her? There's no clue of what's to come. But she was going through a depression, she's told me, and did not seem made to be a diplomat's wife. In April her father had written, *Dearest Rosemary, we are troubled not to have heard from you in so long.* She was the one who had abandoned home and sailed into glamour and peril. The morning after writing this letter, grandfather Herbert had a heart attack in the silence of his deafness, as he stood at the bathroom mirror, shaving.

What I remember: my grandmother Dora coming to stay soon after; standing with Maggy on the hot front walk and sucking a sweet blue popsicle; swinging in Candy Cane City; racing Maggy in slippery new shoes until Maggy skidded into the staircase and split her head open, then the butterfly bandage on her forehead; eating toast buttered with Vegemite while my mother carried drinks to guests at a party; being bundled into a car in the dark as she cried, "We're packing up and leaving!" although she insists that this last is not true. I have no memory of my parents together, which may be why they look so unlikely a pair in those three slides and two photos, which an aunt showed me when I was twenty-three and first went back to Australia.

My husband and I sit in the dark in Germany and gaze at these images, cast upon a bedsheet we've hung over the kitchen's sliding glass doors. This story of my family: It's always felt like my most personal attribute, my worst and best secret, and whenever I meet anyone I might know awhile I need to tell it again. This story was the first I wrote, without even planning to. I was living in New Orleans, trying to be an illustrator while writing grant proposals at Tulane for a living, but found myself one weekend walking to my office, turning on the computer, and trying to push this family out of my ribs all at once as a simple story. That story was too short; it barely began. So I tried turning it into more stories and then a novel, but failed; I tried writing that novel again and again, but each version could not tell this. So I let the octopal story sink into my ribs and wished it would dissolve there, stop climbing into my throat. But it wouldn't, it doesn't, it keeps poking and pushing, and only now that the story seems to have ended can I try again to be free of it, even though my family will not welcome this.

In Germany, when I found the old slides in their metal box and brought them out to show my husband, I was trying to push out the story a new way, by drawing. A color-pencil portrait of my mother as she sits upon a huge whelk on a beach, like a forsaken Venus, surrounded by palms and bottle-brush, the Southern Cross faint in the dark sky behind her. I wanted to draw her young, and to get her nose and mouth right I chose three of my father's 1965 slides and projected the images in the dark bedroom upon sheets of paper taped to the wall. Her slender olive arms, her bright batik dress, her hair, fell as colored light on my hands as I traced her.

With Alex, now, I click through the slides: Maggy laughing in a red snowsuit, me staring at ducks in the Reflecting

Pool, my mother at night in that batik shift, and again in her green bikini. She glows on the bedsheet in our cold German kitchen, larger than we are, the sheet wavering in the window's draft. We gaze up at her and sip our wine. But there's something else in the room as we look at her lit, because you can't sit in the space formed by projector and bright image and not sense the man who took that picture, the man who would be standing with his camera where you now sit with your hand at the carousel. I almost see the current that ran from my father to her as he focused, the energy of his watching like the beam of light that makes her flare to life on the sheet: This stream of watching made what was watched *wanted*. I stare at my glowing mother, her beautiful legs, her neck stretched bare, and imagine my father looking at her even more intently than I do. And then I can only imagine, or fail to imagine, what made him turn away.

The slides spanning my parents' marriage are kept in a flat steel box the size of a board game, where they have been erratically placed in slots, half missing. All are numbered and labeled in my father's hand: *Rosemary, Rosemary and Maggy, Maggy and Jane.* In my mother's hand sometimes, upside down, are more descriptive titles like *Girls on swings* or *Girls in snow* or *Birthday party: before!* Among them is no *Edward*, just one or two *Edward and Maggy*. He took the slides that included him, while my mother kept those of her; they divided the slides of Maggy and me.

The last slide in the box is the final shot of my mother in that marriage. I click to the end of the carousel, and there she is. She stands in her kitchen at night in a yellow swimsuit, hands fisted at hips, chin thrust up, eyes narrowed and smile wide and lurid. She looks Italian or Egyptian, and it seems lascivious to wear a swimsuit in the kitchen at night among half-empty bottles of wine and port. Maybe she'd been dancing the cancan or Charleston, her feet bare on the gritty floor. This picture—not the one with the angel collar and Maggy, and not even the one in the garden, because there she is unconscious—this picture caught her live. But soon it was another part of her my father evidently did not want. It remained in the steel box after he'd taken what he wanted, snapped the clasps shut, moved on.

She wears a brilliant peacock patchwork robe over her swimsuit, shoved back by her fists. Dora had made the robe, sewed each bright piece to the backing with neat black stitches. My mother and I wondered recently what had become of this robe. On the phone, we disagreed about the color of the lining; she said it was red, I said it wasn't, until I said, "Well, I've got it in a picture, hold on."

She said, "Oh, you mean that one of me in my swimsuit vamping for Paul?"

So this picture, the last in the steel box, was taken not in Washington but a few months later in Canberra, one night when the four adults were together. It was not my father who took it, but Paul. And it may catch the first moment of interest, the first fissure before the split. Unless you ponder another small fact: that my parents first met Paul in Washington.

———

In 1965 we returned to Australia, where my father, I am told, was to switch to another department, for my mother. She, Dora, Maggy, and I traveled by train to San Francisco, where we boarded the *Oronsay*. My father flew from Washington shortly after.

As we steamed to Honolulu and Fiji, fashion shows and costume balls filled the time, and for one of these my mother put Maggy and me in a bath of hot cocoa to make our skin brown like South Pacific girls. Maggy was six and I was three. We slipped on grass skirts whose strands tasted bitter, had leis hung around our necks and hibiscus blossoms fixed to our ears and ankles, and went out hand in hand on the shining dance floor. But aside from that chocolate bath and the taste of the skirt, I remember little of this Pacific voyage and wish I did, wish I'd been older, because then I'd imagine it was the first time and I was Cook or Banks looking for the famous southern continent. I'd stand on deck to watch for albatross and see how the stars changed when we crossed the equator, and how the currents changed as well, and when my shadow crept to the other side of my feet, and when water began swirling the other way down the drain: when one pole lost its pull and the other strengthened. To be from the "antipodes" but to have lived on the other side of the world fixes home, the point of orientation, as perpetually elsewhere. The center is never where you are.

When the English first settled Australia, I wonder if it felt to those back home like a parallel world, brimming with light while they slept in darkness, its greenery steaming when frost broke the soles of their boots: an eerie sense of otherness to which they were now yoked, a shadow self. You could stand at Land's End in Cornwall and stare into the Atlantic haze and know that if you sailed straight you'd reach America. But to imagine Australia or New Zealand, you'd have to stare into the grass between your feet and picture someone far down there, staring into the dirt between her own feet, picturing someone like you.

The Maori skull Joseph Banks took back to England he had gotten for a pair of linen drawers, a weird trade — skinned head for empty bottoms — that seems to describe the relations between England and the antipodes: a cynical relation between a smart, old culture and one that's rough, unknowing, like Henry James's great "international theme," although for James the old culture was Europe but the new and naive was America; Australia and New Zealand didn't even come into the picture. But I wonder if it's part of the idea of antipodes that one of the two poles is more powerful, because only one of the two has thought about, imagined, and sought out the other.

In Canberra we returned to the bungalow, which seemed small, even in memory, where houses often swell large. The eucalypt whose pale mottled bark came off in strips stood in the front yard, and at the bottom of the street was a rock where I remember sitting and waiting for my father to come home. Across from the house, a park called Rocky Knob rose up the hill and dropped down the other side, with boulders jutting like dinosaur bones from the dusty grass, magpies shrieking in the cloudy sky.

I turned four in October and went to the Girls' Grammar, to a small shed of a classroom where we colored and napped on mats. When the Queen Mum came to Canberra, the girls at the Grammar tumbled down the hill to wave at her in the motorcade, a plump woman beneath a blue feathered cap. Among the girls who waved were the Stuarts, and I keep trying to see them for the first time. I remember a single moment, struggling with Jenny at the top of the hill, pushing her or being pushed down, but I don't remember when. One day they became relevant: *The Stuart girls are at the Grammar, too. Know them? Patricia and Jenny.*

My parents met the Stuarts at a party they threw, and their parties were marvelous, my mother has told me, written up in Canberra social columns. This one featured white food, which sounds terrible, it sounds German, but knowing the hostess as I have come to, I am sure it was supremely elegant. My parents followed with dinner at our house, another couple along as well.

Then evidently there was a third dinner with just the four, an evening that apparently went like a dream, the night it all must have begun, the first strands unraveling and entwining. The two new couples simply began forming: I see my father and Helen, my mother and Paul, one pair at this end of the table and one at the other, then one at the table and one in the living room, pulled apart and together by gentle currents, both new pairs murmuring and laughing, smoke curling under the bedroom door. It sounds so easy, so natural, these new combinations, everyone fascinated with the new other. It's a strange moment when you look at a new man's face the way you look at your husband's. Orientation shifts:

vertigo. Desire you did not even know you had suddenly envelops you, its object within your grasp. All at once you imagine yourself happy, without having realized how unhappy you'd been. I picture the four the morning after that dinner, dreamy, their ears still humming with the timbre and cadences of the new man or new woman, then looking over the coffee cups to see the wrong one there, and blinking, putting things back to rights.

From then on: outings, always together. *Whoever sees a kangaroo first wins!* We drove into the countryside, cigarette smoke flying out the window. Maggy and I stuck our heads out, too, and opened our mouths to the parching tart wind. In glades of gums, the sun bright and ground baking, when we'd eaten our pasties on the hot wool blankets, one of those four might say to us, "Whoever finds a koala first—Whoever spots the first echidna—Whoever sees a kook."

And my mother would do her kookaburra laugh. She'd rock back on her haunches, shut her eyes, take a breath, and release from her throat a wild pulsing sound, a throbbing shriek that rose through the branches and thin dangling leaves and up into the ancient air, an animal noise that belonged with her platypus toes and made her part of Australia, primitive and wild, a noise that Helen might listen to with a smile, but one I doubt she would ever herself make.

My mother was beautiful, with her strong features and slim limbs, but Helen had a more glamorous, refined beauty. In a 1960s picture of Helen that came up by mistake when my father showed slides years later, a picture that took my breath away, she already possessed what she still has, a style of beauty that seems consciously composed. Recently, on a summer evening in Germany when she and my father had come to visit, she and I went for a walk while our husbands watched the World Cup, and the soft air, the feel of gliding forward in darkness, seemed to make us both transparent and open, make us forget who we were. She told me how she and a girl-friend had traveled together to Europe when she was twenty or so. They sailed second class, but at night they would sneak up to the first-class deck. Well, Jane, she said, laughing; we were good-looking, it was easy to be offered drinks.

She fell in love, she said, with Europe's cultivated beauty, its art. And her own beauty she surely knew how to deploy: how to smile just a little with the pretty teeth and Piero della Francesca lips, how to glance and glance away with the lovely blue eyes, how to reveal modestly her body's splendor.

Not long after that evening walk, as we washed our hands in a restaurant bathroom, she told me that I did not make good use of my beauty. I felt stupid when she said it, sloppy and wrecked beside her in the mirror, and it took two weeks to realize what I think she'd meant: not, as I'd thought, that I dressed badly and had no idea what to do with my hair. But that I did not use my looks to get ahead.

It's awfully superficial, Jane, I know, she'd said, reaching for a towel as she glanced at my reflection with those blue eyes. But these things end up mattering in our world.

My stepfather, her first husband, said to me once, Now there's a woman who's never lost her looks. He narrowed his eyes and almost whistled between his teeth, and I think he was seeing his first wife again, through those forty years since Canberra, since the day he left her, or she left him, or they left each other.

After the eucalypt picnics we'd go back to the Stuarts' house or ours. The four girls would be bathed, Jenny and me pushing at each other's wet pink feet, and then we'd be tucked into bed together. On the other side of the door, Paul and Helen and my mother and father would drink, play music, laugh. At some point they'd come in to kiss us goodnight. I don't know if only our respective parents kissed each of us, or if the others did, too, to be fair—if each of them sat a moment in the dark bedroom, in the quiet, away from the smoke and music and others, and rested a hand lightly on the wrong girl's stomach, and indulged in a private glimpse of a future.

There was a weekend, my mother's told me, when we all drove down to the beach near Canberra and stayed together in a cottage. Another weekend the four adults went to Sydney and checked into a hotel, perhaps with not quite their right names. These points I've been told as facts, uninflected. But everything else bends when I try to get an idea of who did what when. My mother says she heard Helen say to another woman at a party, *There's a man at this party and his name is Edward Cummins and he's mine, so hands off.* Paul says that my father and Helen had a motto: *Screw your courage to the sticking point.* Which might have meant, as he believed, that they were already at it, but might have meant they weren't; they were waiting. My father became furious one night twenty years later and kept saying, *What she did on the bloody ship!* — meaning my mother set the split in motion even before reaching Canberra, perhaps even in Washington. And Helen has said, *Jane, you must understand: I had to get my girls away from Paul.*

I wish I could remember what my mother and Paul said to each other if I slept in the back of his car, or what my father and Helen whispered to each other if I tagged behind on a walk, anything I might have heard or seen, so that I could *know* something, be certain. If nothing more decisive had happened, if the four adults had just dallied and parted, Paul and Helen and Patricia and Jenny would never have remained in my mind, so little trace did they leave.

What traces remain: the tangy hot air as I held my head out of the car window searching for kangaroos and koalas; the lights flashing on as my mother pulled Maggy and me from bed and rushed us outside. And my father as he sat on the edge of my bed with a cigarette and drew glowing orange pictures in the dark, bright circles and swirls like silent fireworks that lingered in the darkness and then slowly dissolved, but lingered still in my eyes after he'd kissed me goodnight, got up, and shut the door.

My sister and I each have copies of the two pictures that record our last day with him. On the back of both of mine he has printed *To Janey with love from Daddy. August 1966,* and this is the start of his transmogrification into photographs and writing. In one photo, the three of us pose beside Lake Burley Griffin, my father kneeling between Maggy and me. I'm in a green-and-red-striped dress with trumpeters on the pockets; my sister's in dark corduroy, black tights, a head-band; my father wears a fawn sweater with a tie knotted in-side. The wintry August sky is clear, pale blue, and all three of us look hopeful. We look like brave pioneers setting off into a new world. In the other picture, we pose on the verandah of a colonial house, and I giggle and press my hand to my mouth. Probably he's pointed out something funny to make us smile. Soon after, he disappeared.

I can't offer a story to prove I loved him. Love describes a relation between one and an other and is only possible when the distinction between yourself and the other is clear, when there's distance. Perhaps if you're too young, love isn't rel-evant. The other is simply crucial, like your own skin, your bones.

Sometime before Maggy and I left Australia came the pres-ents from grandparents and friends: the ink washes of Ab-original girls, the stuffed kangaroo and koala with black rub-ber claws, wooden boomerangs to hang on a wall. There was a night in a hotel or at a friend's when my mother dressed up and I'm guessing she was applying for our U.S. visas, al-though for a long time I understood it as the night she mar-ried Paul. But they didn't marry until later, after we'd lived in Washington a year.

The whole thing had happened in less than nine months. But posts are limited, and Paul's in Canberra was about to end, taking him and his family back over the Pacific. Surely the four had needed to move quickly. Their ability to imagine a new world and step into it dazzles me; they were just thirty-one, thirty-two. And how to resist the miraculous neatness? No one would be left out.

But surely everyone was stunned. The adults, for having done something so astonishing so fast — in 1966 divorce wasn't common, and these divorces were entwined with the men's professional lives and their roles representing countries. And the four girls were stunned, but the way children are: a quiet, numb shock, like a crack in a stone, not enough to split it but inside, silently fissuring.

2

This time we crossed the Pacific by plane, at night, as if in stealth, and as if already the world had grown cold and new, the romantic day of ocean liners gone. Paul had flown earlier and shipped some of our things—dishes, wicker, batik spreads—but until we followed him it apparently wasn't certain that he and my mother would proceed. He talked to her on the phone from Washington and told her she should wait. But she didn't want to wait. She and my father had already divorced, and what could she do now? She applied for a new passport for the three of us, as we could no longer use what we'd had with my father. In this passport we're still called Cummins, and in the group photo my mother's head is tilted, eyes heavily lidded. Maggy stands beside her, alert and troubled, mouth soft. I sit on my mother's lap with her Bellini hand clasping my stomach and grin like a monkey, clueless.

We flew back over our ocean path from Sydney to Honolulu and landed in Los Angeles, where Paul's mother took us to stay in her white bungalow. She and my mother hadn't met, so this surely was awkward—this brand-new woman, not even a wife, and her unknown daughters — all such sudden replacements. My mother called Paul in Washington and insisted he fly out, which he did, but when the two went to dinner they fought, my mother says, and she walked home alone. (Why did they fight? "Oh, just because I went to the French ball after he'd left Canberra. With friends, *mutual* friends of ours.") Not a good start to this new world. But we were there, and how would she support two daughters alone? We flew on to Washington and rented a stone house on Connecticut Avenue, a cold, drafty, leaky house with spiders in the corners, and tried to start new.

Over the next seven years, each couple would establish itself, and each girl would take form. We would live in Washington for three years, first in the uneasy stone house and then a brick one; we'd move to Los Angeles while Paul got a second degree; we'd go on foreign post in South America. My father and his new family would have postings in Asia and the Middle East, so the two families were always on opposite sides of the globe, once a neat 180° apart.

Maggy and Patricia were seven when this new era began, young, but maybe formed enough to have their own soft shapes already, a thin bark. Jenny and I were five and four, just starting, and over those eerie, detached years I think we formed ourselves around the primary facts of the split. I picture cells dividing and subdividing and see us each looking out from within a thin membrane, gathering knowledge and hoarding it, acquiring longings and manners and peculiarities that would become our personal traits. Hurrying this stuff inside, then pushing out layer upon layer of gelatinous skin to keep all of it safe, to keep other things out. Like an oyster wrapping nacreous film around grit, like a tree forming rings of tissue.

When I'd pulled papery strips from the eucalypt by our house in Canberra, it didn't bother the tree. Beneath the bark lay cool blue-white beluga skin, and if you pressed your cheek against it, its tension told you it was alive. In Washington the oaks didn't have smooth skin but ridged crocodile bark that could make your knuckles bleed. But jam a rock into the bark or reach up and snap a green twig, and it bled, too.

In a Miami garden I once saw a slim tropical tree into which someone had stabbed a spade when it was young. The sapling hadn't been mortally hurt, though, it had kept growing, layering tissues and xylem and phloem around the blade, so that the tree's smooth flesh had closed around the spade at its knees, until only the wooden handle showed. I was in my twenties when I saw this, and it reminded me of paintings of saints: a woman standing, head bowed and serene, with the sword that had killed her mortal self piercing her ribs; another with the ax that had severed her head from her trunk lodged lovingly in her neck, rimmed with a demure line of blood. Saints and their attributes, a complicated symbiosis, the saints held forever in the moment that cleaved them from mortal life and gave them life eternal. The saints don't actually caress the sword, ax, or rock, just live with it deeply. That's what the Coconut Grove tree looked like, with its flesh enveloping the spade. It needed that spade now; you could not draw it out. It's how I grew up, and how

I imagine Jenny did, too, with our parents' split at our core, our tissues growing around it, around the fact that we'd each been replaced.

I wonder sometimes how our lives would have been if the conditions had been more enlightened or less international: if instead of oceans and half a globe between us, there'd been only a park and a few streets, so we could see our counterparts on weekends, and they hadn't become so fantastic. Or if those four parents had been more modern, versed in psychology, and, worrying about the effects of this rearrangement, had made enormous efforts to heal the little rips.

As I write this, though, I know I prefer how it was done. I like the austerity, the extremity. It gave us, or I know it gave me, a secret, black, precious possession, like when you split open a geode and find the sharp crystals inside. For seven years we may have seemed like ordinary girls kicking balls and learning to write and getting our hair cut and skinning our shins. But inside each of us was crystallizing a mass of fantasy, jealousy, and longing that was crucial and would define us.

These things happen: A father vanishes overnight and turns into paper. Another man appears, his face rough and smelling of cigarettes and scotch when we kiss him, but he's not ours, this is understood, he belongs to a pair of girls somewhere else. Our own identity — as fixed by name, father, nationality — is as curiously cloudy as the cigarette smoke that drifts around him when he sits on the sofa or drives fast through Rock Creek Park. And this problem of identity begins to fix on the facts not only that our own father has left us, but that we each have a double, a girl we cannot see but this new nonfather sees each time he looks at us. He sees through our eyes straight to her.

Paul had a sixties style, dark hair, Beatle boots. He was tall, walked with a swagger, and had eyes so dark they seemed almost without pupils, and a mouth that in pictures looks as soft as Paul McCartney's, but wasn't. He parted his thin hair to the side, and even then it receded from his forehead, which was tanned from tennis and lined from raising his brows in disbelief, from not giving a good goddamn about something as insignificant as the sun. He smoked and drank steadily but never seemed to alter; his own father had left when he was a boy; he believed in picking yourself up by the bootstraps. He had a fast, gunshot laugh.

Brought from his first life and now in that leaky Connecticut Avenue house: a low-slung black leather Mies van der Rohe chair; a tough leather table from Peru; a carved whale's tooth, cold and heavy in my hands, with a gleaming dark mother-of-pearl where the tooth had been rooted in the whale's jaw. Also the double bed he had shared with Helen, where he now slept with my mother, and that would later be given to me. Paul drove an old smoke-gray Jaguar and had a large framed photograph of a snarling tiger taken so close you could see each strand of fur, the gleam of saliva on its fangs, the black pupils in its wild green eyes. At dinner I'd stare into those mad, slanting eyes, and this tiger, the Jaguar, the leather chair and table, the whale's tooth: All these things configured Paul. This jungle would grow when we moved to his mother's house in L.A. and then on to South America: the saber-toothed tiger trapped in the tar pit, its kin who ranged over the isthmus of Panama and killed off the old, gentle sloths, the wild German shepherd Paul got to protect us but whose nails left bloody lines in our legs — and the sharks, all the gray sharks I have never in life seen but that glide every month through my dreams.

I don't remember thinking about Paul when we first moved into that cold stone house, just being conscious of him as a large living fact, a figure whose dark form took up space. And not just his form but his low voice, his whistle, the smoke gusting from his nose. I sat in that windy living room, staring out at cars and buses and worrying to the point of panic about not being able *not* to think, about the fact that there was always something in my head, like choking: numbers, pictures, words, even if they were just *Don't think don't think don't think.* So I had room in there for thinking. Just not about a man like Paul, or about the shock of what had happened.

He went downtown each day to the State Department, and Maggy and I walked down Connecticut to Murch Elementary, Maggy to second grade and me to kindergarten. We still called ourselves Cummins, we still were Australian, we still had bright little Aussie accents. Cars and buses rushed down the wrong side of the street, and it was autumn when in Canberra it had been spring; the world felt mirrored, unreal. There was a spell that first year when in bed at night I'd watch lights careen through my window, dance up the wall to the ceiling, then race down the other wall whenever a car passed. I'd stare at them without blinking, stare at one dancing cluster of lights after another, and try to be hypnotized. But at a certain moment I'd begin to tremble, then cry, then shake with sobs, pillow jammed in my face until it was slimy. I'd turn it over and go to sleep and every night dream the same dream: of flying back to my father. Through the airplane's window I'd peer through Canberra's marbled clouds and see him tiny and far on the tarmac. His figure would grow as the plane descended, until we landed, the hatch swung open, and I jumped into his arms and clung like a monkey, at which point the dream stopped, because what on earth could happen next?

After this came a time when it seemed I was never awake but suspended, dreaming, in ice or glass. A sense of being off-kilter: Home, the real center, was far away, and the feel of hovering at an edge was sickening. I did what people said to do, pinched my arm hard, but a pinch in a dream felt like a real one, so there didn't seem to be any point.

How do you make your self home? Are *people* your home? Does loving or needing someone make him home for you? A feeling that's gravitational: Wherever he is, is home. The one toward whom you helplessly gravitate and near whom you feel settled, that painful yearning dissolved. When you're a child, surely your parents are home. Fathers and fatherlands, the sun. A basic sense of orientation, of knowing where the sun is.

My father stayed in Canberra for several months after we left, and then he was posted in Asia. By then both divorces were settled, and Helen and my father married, as did my mother and Paul, as if the split had blasted apart stones and fused the pieces, making metamorphic families.

Over the next years letters flew between Paul and his girls and between Daddy and us; letters even between us and the girls, although I forgot about these until finding them years later in a box in my mother's basement. First, when I was too young to write, I drew my father pictures: little girls in long bright dresses, small boys falling from trees. My mother wrote for me once, but apparently it was made clear that a letter in her hand was unwelcome; only the men, of the four adults, were to communicate. Maggy and I didn't talk to our father on the phone those seven years, and I do not know why: because it was expensive and no one made such calls in those days, or no one thought of it, or maybe because a live line between the two households seemed dangerous, fire.

Our father wrote us together, *Dear Maggy and Jane,* Maggy first presumably because she was older, and it must have been hard for him to decide what to say. He described exotic places, local customs and shows. *Some of the riders looked like the Saracens who fought against the Crusaders (have you read about them?) with turbans and cloaks that streamed behind them when the horses galloped . . .* He made observations about the time of year and what we might be up to: *I suppose you've had lots of snow and fun with your sled and snow saucer. Is that what it's called?* The other girls are always present: *I know how quickly Patricia and Jenny are changing now and I expect you are too . . . The next birthdays are yours Jane and Jenny's too on the same day.* He signed with variations of *I think of you often and love you. Your*

Father. Below this he'd print a double row of *X*'s: at first five *X*'s, until after a few letters he settled on three but matched it with a double row of three *O*'s. A birthday card to just one of us would have a single row of *X*'s and *O*'s.

He sent presents for birthdays and Christmas, fabulous things from Asia that would appear in the front hall wrapped in battered brown paper and smelling dry and foreign. Inside: a little leather pouch containing tiny ivory tigers and birds; an intricately wrought silver elephant that looked seamless but split neatly apart in your hands; a fine silver pin in the shape of a peacock with tiny whorling filigree feathers; a heavy wooden jewelry box to put the peacock in, one box for Maggy, one for me. The wood was dark and glossy, as dense as gold, and inlaid with brass scrolls and arabesques that on the curved lid surrounded our names, *Margaret, Jane.* The box opened with a small brass key, and inside sat a shelf trimmed in red velvet, which you could lift to reveal a lower, secret layer. I carried this heavy treasure, the silver peacock, and the plump silver elephant to Show and Tell, then installed them on my dresser. They were proof, proof that was splendid but hurt.

The letters often came the same day: one for Paul, one for us, nothing for my mother. Paul would take the letter from his girls and read it in private with a scotch; Maggy and I read ours from our father together in one of our bedrooms. We called our father Daddy in our letters but didn't say the word much. The girls also called our father Daddy, while their own father they called Father. We called their father Paul. The girls were called the girls, or Paul's girls, his real girls.

————

The parallels between the two families were so neat we seemed as designed as nature, twinned markings on the wings of a moth. My father's birthday came a week before Paul's, so Maggy and I wrote cards for both men together. My mother's birthday fell two weeks before Helen's; Jenny's birthday was the same as my own. In April 1968, two years after the split, my father and Helen had a baby boy, and four days later, so did my mother and Paul. Nicholas and Tommy: two babies that consolidated the new marriages and knotted us tighter. Tommy bound Maggy and me by blood to Paul and the girls, and bound the girls to our mother; Nicholas bound us even more to the girls as well as to Helen, and bound the girls to Daddy. Like paper dolls all holding hands.

Something else we shared with the girls: grandparents. What the old people thought of the rearrangement I don't know; they seemed to accept it, stalwart. The girls' grandmother was Elsie, a petite woman with a face like an elderly movie star, a smoker's dry voice, long thin fingers, a husky laugh, and a very old cat named Shadow, who could open the kitchen door. Her manner was gentle, and when we told her something she enjoyed she'd open her eyes wide and say, "Oh, *my-y-y*," then shake lightly with a papery laugh. If she resented that we'd displaced her real granddaughters, she never let Maggy and me know. Every birthday and Christmas she'd send a card and check for $10, and during the year we lived in her house in L.A., she never let us think we were anything but her own. How did those girls feel, knowing we were in their grandmother's house, leaning against her knee, getting her birthday checks, earning her laughter?

Probably how we felt knowing they now had our Maisie

and Albert. Our grandparents had begun writing us at once after the split, sweet, passionate letters that began *Darling Janie, My dearest Janie, Oh! Janie!* They'd each write a part, and Maisie would sign, *all my love—<u>lovingly</u>!* and beneath that squeeze as many *X*'s and *O*'s as could fit in the last sliver of paper, wild squashed *X*'s that turned corners and jammed into words, like she was kissing you all over your face.

Albert and Maisie traveled to Asia and sent us cheery postcards reporting their adventures with rickshaws and spices and giving news of our father, without mentioning those other girls in his house; they must have known children can get sick with jealousy. When we read these postcards, we'd never have imagined them with those girls, not realized our grandparents had made the trip in order to meet and start loving them. But at the same time our father wrote that he and Helen looked forward to having his parents stay with the girls, while he and she got away on their own, and reading this letter even now I'm jealous. My mother tells me that Albert wrote her, too, saying they'd met their new daughter-in-law and liked her very much: how this had stung. I can't but wonder if they were instructed to do this, if those two old people sat at the kitchen table in their bluestone villa in South Australia pondering the matter, wading anxiously in the ocean of difficult protocol into which they'd suddenly been cast. *Marriage,* Albert wrote me years later in his watery blue hand, *is meant to last a lifetime.*

The absent presence of the other family was never mentioned but always felt, a sense of otherness elsewhere to which we were bound. The sun wasn't over us just now because it was over them. Or a sense of all of us holding our breath, and maybe the arrangement might work. It had to: Everything was fair and right, because everything was even. It was fair that there was a Jenny somewhere who had my birthday and father and grandparents and half brothers, because, after all, I had hers. The letters she sent me, which I found recently in a plastic pouch labeled *Friends,* tell of horses, judo lessons, swim meets, new clothes. Her writing is pretty and plump, with little hearts for O's, and she signs off *I love you and miss you very much!* I expect I wrote the same things to her and signed off that way, too.

It seems strange, though, when we could hardly remember each other, and impossible that we could *miss* each other when we'd parted ways at four and five and the circumstances were rough. Even more unlikely when I think of how it would be when we'd meet again: how we'd look at each other in Jenny's pink bedroom and see only the girl who'd taken everything. So I wonder how these letters began, whose idea they were. No one on our side seemed up to that sort of decorum. Maybe the wish was to turn us into friendly pen pals, little paired animals of a zoo or an ark, cheery written proof that the enterprise was working. Surely the hope, anyway, was that the arrangement would be fine, that the four adults could brush hands clean and smile and shake and say, "See, then, no harm done!"

I went to first grade, then second; we moved to a house on Barnaby Street, where we'd return when I was eleven and where most of my dreams are still staged. A half-timbered brick house, fairy-tale, gothic, giant oaks along the sidewalk, shaggy firs at either side, a concrete path leading through grass limp and silky as hair. Pink azaleas grew beneath the front windows among tangled ivy, ferns, and fat silver slugs; daddy longlegs waited on the front steps and trash cans, waited to run up your legs and arms.

By the time we reached Barnaby my father was a shadow, a function of light or thought; he was gone. The fabulous gifts he sent were solid, but you could look at them and hold them and nothing would happen, there was no secret message in the velvet lining of the jewelry box or in the belly of the silver elephant, no matter how you poked and shook them. He was not even a voice. And neither were we: invisible and silent. We could send nothing but paper to make him *see* us, nothing but letters, pictures, gold stars stuck on schoolwork. We'd hurl this stuff halfway around the world, but it was dead by the time it reached him.

And his blue-ink words were dead on the page by the time he folded each letter and slid it into an envelope, sealed it, addressed it, licked the stamps and placed them on the corner, slipped the envelope in his breast pocket, took it with him in the car to the Australian Embassy, and mailed it, and it flew over the Pacific and the Rockies and the Mississippi River until it reached Washington, then fell through the brass slot in the heavy oak door and was picked up by my mother and looked at a moment, then propped smartly for us against an Indonesian figurine on the orange chest. By the time Maggy and I had slit open the envelope and read the letter, his words were dead. And no matter how much you looked at them, they only said what they said, sentences about Nicholas and the heat and always Patricia and Jenny, something missing even though he seemed fond. A phantom limb, not there but aching.

Whereas Paul was actually there. He would stride from the Jaguar, eyes straight ahead as he moved fast up the sidewalk, whistling low. He'd come through the screen door and stand there, regard the state of the house. Sometimes he'd keep whistling in the kitchen as he fixed a drink — he whistled with arabesques like smoke — and if so, that was lucky. He'd tell jokes that night, horror stories. In the living room with a scotch, or at dinner, he'd imitate a shark to terrify us. His pupilless eyes were utterly focused, and even his nose tilted up like a shark's. He'd stare dead ahead and pull down his mouth until he looked vacant, a monster, and glide and suddenly lunge, twist his head, and rip. But it was funny, a terrifying sort of funny. In a low, conspiratorial voice he told us about a boy attacked by a shark in the San Francisco Bay as he swam with his girlfriend, and how first the shark ripped off the boy's left leg, then his right, then his left arm, then his right, and his girlfriend clutched him under the chin and kept swimming to shore — until finally when she reached the sand, all she held was the boy's bleeding head.

He told stories about the Abominable Snowman, his face shuddering and eyes bulging as he simply said the name, or about a man with a hook instead of a hand, or about the hand itself that had been cut off but could still move, alive. Paul would lay his own hand on the table and drop a napkin over his wrist to isolate it, then jerk his fingers in little spasms, and stare down at them, horrified, and I'd get carried away and scream. Then he'd laugh and return the napkin to his lap and keep eating. He'd go back to the original subject, Humphrey or Nixon or some jackass in the department, but then in a pause, as he chewed, he might notice us still sitting there and get back to the shark.

"So do you know what to do," he might say, dead serious, "if you see a shark coming your way? If you're out in the water, swimming way the hell out there, and you see a big fin gliding your way?" He'd wait for an answer, brows high, expectant.

I had no idea. I didn't even like having my legs under the table.

"No? Well, I'll tell you." He'd put down his knife and fork, lean forward, lower his voice. "Here's what you do. You wait until that big fin is almost there, wait until he's *just about got you*. Keep an eye on him, though. You don't want a mistake. Then at the last minute, at the very last minute — you twist around fast and grab his fin," and he twisted and grabbed in his chair to demonstrate, his eyes squinting across the sea.

"Then what?"

"You ride!"

"But then what?"

He shrugged. Who cared? The best part was over.

This was good humor. Otherwise, when he came in the door, after he'd gone to the kitchen and tossed a few ice cubes into a glass and poured a good inch of scotch, he'd return to the living room, jiggling his glass, and position himself on the sofa. He'd snap open the paper or switch on the news or read one of the letters from his girls, the real girls, and if you happened to come near or make a noise, he'd stop and stare as if he had no idea who the hell you were or what the hell you were doing there. If you said nothing worth hearing, he'd turn away: no patience for losers or fools. But if you said something clever he might lift a brow and take interest. And if you said something downright daring, he'd laugh, and those dark eyes would linger on your face, consider you: as if you might just be worth his while. And that current of interest was the start of everything, the current that lit me to life.

In that same room, on that striped brown sofa where Paul would sit and regard me — on that sofa when I was sixteen, I sat with a boy in the dark, a boy who wasn't the one I loved but who had come over one night to try his luck, and he put his arm around me, laughed, and softly sang: *Jane, if you can't be with the one you love, love the one you're with.* So I lay back and let him slide his hands under my shirt, let him hold my breasts, kiss my neck, suck so hard the blood nearly broke through the skin, a pain that soothed, and I pretended not to care that he wasn't the one, because by then finding such replacements seemed natural.

At the beginning, Maggy tried to please Paul, but soon she didn't bother. An incident I've been told: Walking with him one day in Washington, through a park or down a street, Maggy, seven, put her hand up to be held. He slipped his own hand in his pocket.

Was he thinking of his real girls? Trying to stay true?

Another incident, again his hand, but this moment Maggy and I both remember: We sat in Paul's old Jag while he went to the post office or liquor store, and, restless, Maggy found a Red Hot in the glove compartment and gave it to me to try. When he came back and saw me sucking, he turned to Maggy, demanded to know, and she said, Someone threw it in the window! He slapped her leg fast, a slap that left a hand burning on her skin for days, forever, it burns there still, and this moment—the car, Paul's face, that red-hot hand—established relations among us. I was the cute one, the baby: preferred. He would never slap me.

Maybe she was old enough to stay true to Daddy, or maybe she didn't need to fix herself on one father or the other. She was slim, tall, with a boyish haircut and one blue eye and one green (*You look just as darling as I expected and hoped and you certainly are growing tall, too,* wrote Daddy. *It's hard to believe that in two more birthdays you're going to be a terrible teenager. But not* too *terrible, I hope*). Around Paul, she put her head down, slid away, made herself not care if he liked her or not. She made things. Daddy sent her origami paper, beautiful squares of glossy colors, and she'd sit cross-legged with the tip of her tongue at the corner of her mouth and fold lime and magenta and indigo squares until they became parrots or swans. Later she'd make candles, pouring layers of different colored wax into a milk carton, and when the wax had hardened she'd peel the carton away, and there stood a block of rainbow.

She didn't care if Paul liked her, but I did. You can imagine the moon on the other side of the world, but what about the sun above you? Paul would look down now and then, consider me. He seemed pleased with the gold stars stuck on my schoolwork. He seemed to like that I was the little blond princess in the play, memorized the whole damned thing, and shouted the frog's lines when he forgot them. And that when a boy kissed me I pushed him down the playground steps, and that I had rope-burn welts all over my arms but never said uncle. He said these things were terrific and tousled my hair. He liked a cute smart kid who acted tough.

I reminded him, my mother said, of Jenny.

Two things happened within the first years of the split to articulate the realliances. The first involved our names. How it happened I don't know, and neither my sister nor my mother remembers, but what I picture is this: One day a letter from the girls came for Paul, but it was addressed not from Patricia and Jenny Stuart but from Patricia and Jenny Cummins. They had taken our name, or our father had given it. I picture a moment of seasickness, seeing my name in another girl's hand, worrying that our father had adopted those girls, that to do this he'd given us up, so whose were we? I might have asked Maggy about it in the attic, slithering around the floor in an old crinkled taffeta dress of my mother's. But probably not, as I would not ask my mother, because the rearrangement somehow wasn't our business; it was just the air, breathe it or not.

I also don't know how Paul reacted to his girls' dropping his name and taking our father's, leaving him just as

Helen had. It was probably one of those nights of broken glass, smoke, slamming doors, my mother sleeping curled in the car.

What I do know is that one morning I went to the principal's office and said to a woman peering over a typewriter, "I'm not Jane Cummins anymore. Now I'll be Jane Stuart." A necessary trade: my Barbie for your skates. Those girls had my name and father. I'd need theirs.

It didn't happen legally. I was still Cummins on most envelopes and report cards until 1969, although sometimes also Stuart. Then Cummins disappeared. My sister took Paul's name, too, although I doubt she wanted to, as I did; more likely my mother urged her, icing to hide the lumps. My father never mentions the changed names in the letters I have, and by 1969 he was addressing his envelopes to Misses M. and J. Stuart, and as I write this now I can't help but wonder: What if I was the one who switched names first?

The second thing that happened was this, and it's less a moment than the speculation of one. I'm the one who kept our father's letters, the folded sheets with his blue handwriting flowing across the page. You'd think Maggy would have kept them, she was older and closer to him, and even now her basement in Chicago is so full of papers and CDs and records and beads you'd think she'd never thrown anything out. But she didn't keep those letters; I put them in a plastic pouch labeled *Daddy,* and, whenever we moved, I packed the pouch in a box, then unpacked it to add the new letters that came. I found this pouch decades later, in a box in my mother's basement, each letter still folded as my father had folded it and still in its neatly slit envelope.

In one envelope, though, I found not just a letter but pictures I don't remember seeing; usually the photos he sent he'd marked to Maggy or me, or we divided them and put them in our scrapbooks. These pictures showed Daddy and his new family, composed color pictures he must have taken with a tripod and timer. Surely it was strange for Maggy and me, at ten and eight, to get a letter from our father and slip from the envelope glossy color images of him posing with his new boy on his knee, as he had posed with us by Lake Burley Griffin. Or pictures of his new family arrayed in a garden, the lovely young mother with bouffant hair holding her lacy new baby, those two other girls in party dresses smiling at their new brother, the handsome man in shirtsleeves and thin tie happily regarding his new family, all together in a garden, somewhere else. There would be many more pictures like this, Jenny or Patricia on the arm of my father's chair, leaning into him, smiles all around. I don't know what we felt when we saw the first of these. A flare of panic so cold it must be stifled at once: *You have been replaced.*

We didn't put these pictures in any album, not Maggy's with the blue and brown batik cover or my big green one with the soft pages falling out. Either she or I tucked them back into the envelope with Daddy's letter, which was dated December 1969. It ends like this: *The little colour photo was on Nicholas's first birthday; that and the other two showing Nicholas are for you two. Please give the other three (which I have marked to him) to your Daddy. With lots of love, Your Father.*

So names slid around; attachments were understood to have properly shifted. That letter with those pictures either Maggy or I slipped back in the envelope, and then I put that envelope in the plastic pouch, and when we packed to leave Washington for Los Angeles, or Los Angeles for South America, I put the pouch carefully in a box, and then a closet, and then a basement, the casual documents of our realliance.

And Paul? Maybe one day after he regarded a glossy image of his girls leaning at the knee of that man who now had both them and Helen — or maybe one day after I'd first printed his name beside mine on dotted green lines — maybe he looked down at me and saw a little ally, a small consolation. And what I have wondered since and still wonder now is whether there was a moment between us, a silent agreement: *I will be yours if you will be mine. We will replace, and punish, those others.*

When I try to imagine Jenny then, on the other side of the world, I do something a man taught me at college about playing pool. To hit a ball off the side into a pocket, look at the pool table and imagine a mirror version alongside the real one. Aim for the pocket in the mirror version. So I imagine that other family over there, Jenny growing up like me: picking up a letter from her father that my father had brought home from the embassy, sliding her finger under the seal, reading it on her stomach in her bedroom, putting the paper down on the pillow, staring at the palm tree out the window, wondering what to do with the ache, the panic that feels like your insides might slip out, the unvoiced question of whether she'd see her invisible father again, and what would happen when she did; and the haunting sense of that other girl over there, the one like her who now had him.

Moving a lot as a child means you keep starting over from nothing, proving yourself again and again. It's like being a thin sandy solution and, by fierce will, *making* that solution congeal around you. And the more you move to alien places the more often you have to do this, like being dropped into acids that dissolve you each time. Personal traits need to be asserted in each new place, which means contests must be waged and won. If you've worked hard to become anything — fastest runner, best skater, funniest girl, anything — these terms have melted into your skin, become your skin, and must be preserved. If you stay in one place, your standing and self are only threatened when a new, outside girl appears. But if you keep being new; and your name is new and must be practiced, embarrassing, on dotted lines; and your father is new, although it's never clear whether you should write down both fathers or add the word *step* or just pretend he's really yours; and your nationality is new, to be checked in the right box, not the wrong one, as if you had no clue what you were: Then the attributes that are truly *yours* — fastest, best, smartest — are crucial. To take them away is like ripping off skin. So on top of the split and the jealousy it engendered, all the moving and remaking made us bitterly competitive as a matter of course.

When I've done the pool trick to imagine those other girls being like us, it's partly right: We could not have shared more. But it's also wrong. On that side there seemed to be more consciousness — more consciousness about *us*. Maybe because the girls were older and nearer each other in age, more allied, not split the way Maggy and I were by my sidling over to Paul. Or maybe because that family seemed to have solidified so firmly, which gave them a fixed place from which to look out and think hard and talk about us, the others.

One day those girls did something novel: With their letter to Paul they sent a tape. We gathered in the living room to listen. The reels whirred, ice clinked in Paul's glass, the springs of my mother's gold chair squeaked as she shifted.

Then suddenly the girls' voices broke into the air. "Hello, Father," they said with bright Aussie accents. There was giggling, then music, and they began to sing:

"Imagine there's no heaven . . ."

I lay on the brown and gold rug, combing the dirty tassels, sick. My mother watched Paul, whose face grew hard as he listened, one hand gripping his scotch glass and the other dead still on the armrest.

"We hope someday you'll join us . . ."

Paul looked then at the alien world around him, the woman and girls who had displaced his real ones. My mother's face stiffened. She probably sat back in the gold chair, crossed her legs, and sipped her martini, but sooner or later something unfortunate was said, and Paul got up, switched off the recorder, and took it with another drink to the bedroom. All that night and for days we heard the girls' voices and that song through the door while my mother slept on the sofa or out in the car. And why hadn't we thought of it, why had we let the girls do it first?

At about the same time, they sent one of those pictures of themselves in a tropical garden, sitting side by side among palm trees, banana plants, bright flowering shrubs. Their hands lie in their laps, and their faces are soft—but their eyes stare into the camera, intent. Jenny's are deeply shadowed. Each girl holds her head at a tilt, Patricia to the left, Jenny to the right, each with her hair falling along her face in a wave. Patricia wears a flowered green shift; Jenny wears pale pink. With the grass beneath them and banana leaves and shrubs behind, they look like blossoms springing up from the grass, blossoms whose roots would, if they could, plunge incredibly deep and reach clear to the other side of the globe, clear to their father, our house.

I wonder who they're looking at. My father, kneeling before them on the grass with his camera, as he'd knelt before us? Or straight through him, through the lens, at their own father? Or are they looking hard at all of us on our side of the world, as if they have the power to see?

Usually those photos have a notation on the back in my father's hand, as he'd annotated the ancient slides. When I found this picture recently, I turned it over, like I used to push my fingers into the velvet corners of the jewelry box, searching for a message I'd missed. On the back of this photo the girls had written: *M + J HERE WE ARE FIERCE P + J.*

———

Sometimes I wonder what it would be like not to have jealousy running in my veins. It's like fuel, gaseous, and if you strike the right match, I flame. I can be jealous of anything. *Jealousy, jalousie,* a shuttered blind, Venetian blind, both words from Latin for *zeal,* and I picture the zealot's ravening eyes. So much of jealousy seems held in the image of the Venetian blind and those eyes: peering through the slats, not seeing enough, seeing too much, shadows falling in obscuring stripes, not being there but outside, looking in. Jealousy is as rich as weather and takes on different forms. One is to observe the person you love with the other; another is to be unable to see this but *know* it's happening, far away, know that you're being displaced. The heart of jealousy: knowing you're dispensable.

So it's not true that these shadowing years, when the two families didn't see each other or speak, traced no drama. I think a silent struggle raged between the distant girls, to make up for what had been lost or taken, not to be displaced.

When a solid body enters or floats upon water, a corresponding volume of liquid is removed: displacement. The summers we lived in Washington we went to the Delaware shore. We'd gone there with Daddy when we'd been in Washington with him, and now, in 1969, when I was seven and Maggy was ten, we went with Paul. It's a beach where Paul still has a house, the beach where I got married; it feels more like home than any place.

Each morning the lifeguards dragged their white wooden stands from the boardwalk toward the water, each to his own stretch of beach bordered by rock jetties. His chair in place, he'd dive into the waves to test the currents, then post a red or yellow flag and plant orange buoys in the sand.

Paul would lean back on his towel with a beer and the paper and watch the waves until they looked right for riding. Then he'd saunter down to the water and through the froth, dive into a rising curl, emerge where the water was smooth. There he'd tread, his head dark, looking out to sea. When a good wave swelled forward, he'd turn and stroke hard until he entered its pull, stiffen like a board, and ride it in. I'd stand ankle deep and watch him, watch his dark face and arms glide forward in the glossy underside of the wave, come toward me in the rushing froth.

When he'd had enough he would stand and nod at me, and I'd splash forward, follow him back in; he wanted to teach me to swim. When it got too deep for me to walk or the waves kept knocking me over, he'd tow me to the other side of the waves, out to where it was glossy and deep. I'd clutch him tight. He'd hold me for a time and we'd rise with the swells, float up with a wave until we seemed as high as the blue water tower, it seemed we gazed far down at the beach and bright umbrellas and lifeguards and people on towels: alone with him, lofty. In lulls between waves, he'd teach me to swim. He'd have me lie on his hands and practice kicking. There'd be a pause while he held me and we floated, waited. Then suddenly, with no warning I can remember, he'd hurl me into the deep water. As I thrashed to try to reach him, he'd fix his eyes on mine but swim backward, deeper, his face gliding away.

When I'd finally fought hard enough to earn the right not to drown, he'd look pleased at how quickly I got it, and he'd reach out, draw me in. "That's the way, Pookala. The only way to learn."

The cottage we'd rented was red and white and tiny, crammed with magazines, dolls, china animals, junk. It was hot. In our cots it was like being at the beach still, baking, there was so much sand in our sheets and hair. One morning Maggy and I escaped before anyone was up. The tough grass glistened with dew, and sunlight slanted through the beach mist. No one was out; the road was sandy and quiet. Maybe we'd planned this. Maybe we'd arranged it with the girl next door, because she appeared on the grass, and together we crossed the bleached road and walked to the beach.

It was too early for the lifeguards, but we weren't going to swim. We'd just wade, let our feet sink into dissolving holes and feel the hermit crabs tickling. We stood in our bathing suits, sudsy water fanning toward us in sheets. Sunlight shone through the green water as a wave rose, then it crashed, and surf scudded toward us, pulled at our feet as it slid back out. We stood still, sinking deeper into the sand with each rush, until we were planted, and teetered.

After a while I tugged my feet from the sucking sand and waded in to rinse my legs. But something happened: There's a black break in the sequence and what I know next is that I'm far out in the ocean, so far that the blue water tower is tiny. I try to stand, but my feet jab into nothing, and I go under. Then there's shocking silence, darkness, a drumming pain in my head, no knowledge of where the sun is. I spin, arms and legs loose in the depth. At last I come up, gasping, but with nothing to hold go under again, swallowing water, breathing water, and I do this again and again until slashing now I clutch something solid. The girl next door, come to save me. Though she's Maggy's age, she's as small as I am, and when I clutch her head to pull myself up, I push her under. So she claws at my neck until she comes up and it's me who's pushed back into that silence of bursting lungs, until then I fight my way up again. I clutch her face, poke her eyes, pull at her ears and hair. I push her matted head down so I can come up. Then her nails dig into my shoulders, her knees jab my stomach, until she comes up and I go under, until I break into the air again, gasping, and with her hair tangled in my hands push her down. And on it goes, a nightmare I still have, until Maggy reaches us, and with her the lifeguards, who grab us and pull us in and lay us out on the sand and want to know our names, and where are our parents.

It wasn't Jenny in the water that day, but a girl whose name I no longer know. But this is what it would be like with Jenny and me when we meet at twelve and eleven. As if our family were a watery element in which only one of us could stay afloat, and to live you must displace the other.

Nine years later, Jenny and I came to this beach. She was seventeen, I was sixteen, and she had just crossed the Pacific to live with her father. He invited me along to his beach house — to keep Jenny company, to protect him, who knows.

While we were there, on an afternoon when I had done the sort of thing it seemed I had to do to her and she had been left alone, she wrote a note to herself, a diary entry, which I either found and took or she gave me.

I'm just telling you one thing. Don't ever leave yourself behind. Because you lose yourself in the process — somewhere in the middle of the Pacific or something . . .

Sadness has nothing to do with it. You have to be indifferent — well — you have no choice anyway because you're lost.

3

Jean Rhys, who was born in Dominica of white Welsh stock but later lived in London, once said, "Am I an expatriate? Expatriate from where?" She belonged no more in England than she had at "home" in the Caribbean: *white cockroach.* Another writer, Caryl Phillips — born in Saint Kitts of African blood but raised in Britain — said he's from a point of water in the Atlantic. Where we're from, where home is supposed to be, seems so nebulous, at the intersection of blood and place.

Jenny was born in South America, Maggy in Southeast Asia, places that I think have meant little to them. By ten and eight, Maggy and I had changed names and nationalities and had lost our accents as well, and these things have so much to do with who you are. We couldn't say convincingly where we were from. I don't know what the other girls did, but Maggy and I laughed and shrugged when anyone asked, and still do.

Don't ever leave yourself behind. A plain sentence, like *Make yourself home.* Syntax that's simple but suggests so much more: This self, this thing you start making when you're small, is both a physical body and vaporous, unfixed, because it *can* be left behind, and might never be home.

By the time we left Washington for Los Angeles in 1969, and then left L.A. for South America in 1970, "home" was a vanishing point behind us, a place figured by our father, the Australian emu-and-kangaroo seal that appeared sometimes on his letters, and our grandparents. The old stuffed kangaroo and koala they'd given us sat molting on our dressers, relics; and a whiff of that lost world rose from Albert and Maisie's letters — a sense of a young country still being settled. "Prevent bush fires!" cried the envelopes, and the stamps showed possum or cockatoo, paintings called *On the Wallaby Track* or *The First Fleet*. When I was eight I would look at those stamps, gaze at the emu-and-kangaroo seal, and feel a weird mix of aching homesickness and fakery in claiming a place I did not even know.

Letters from Britain to the first of our line in Australia, a hundred and fifty years ago, close, *I remain with kindest love to all . . . Give my kind love to Papa.* Such quiet potency, almost a prayer, so hopeful that the words will be read with eyes and a heart still living, when so much ocean and time stretch between writer and reader. *With all my love! Lovingly!* Maisie signed her letters to us. But we were the ones who'd flown to an unknown world, not even a land but a condition of floating, the strange new world our parents had made.

During the seven years after the split, we lived in five houses — two in Washington, Elsie's bungalow in Los Angeles, a yellow villa in South America, and one other — but they were just houses, not homes. We didn't own them but shed them when we moved on. *Home* or *house*: *Home* seems roomier, more feel than structure. Yet even *house* can mean more than a building, the House of Windsor, House of Atreus. House can be a synecdoche, can describe both the structure and those who live in it, the breath, blood, and flesh pacing its hallways, held under the father's name like a roof. Fatherland, father, and house: ways of knowing who you are, where you're from.

It's also in the idea of the house that those seven years were as tense, I think, as in the unspoken struggle between the girls: the fear that it would become plain that one of the couples had made a mistake, one of the new houses would fall.

The couples had surely watched each other since Canberra, a watching that I imagine turned intense and oblique with half a globe between them and communications made of paper. Just how happy were those other two? Each couple had photos to work from, clues we girls gave in our letters, the communiqués of the men. Both couples dwelled in the world of diplomacy, after all, where cool surfaces are scrutinized for signs of inner weakness. So many points of comparison and competition: the career paths of the men; how accomplished and smart each girl was turning out, crucial proof of each new couple's success; the progress of the baby boys, emblems of the new marriages that invited a return to the most intimate moments of the dead ones.

Diplomacy is nothing without presentation. And tucked into the letters from the other side of the world, those poised photos presented a family as blossoming as the gardens.

Whether the happy images were true, I don't know, but they seeped into our brains. That was the *real* family. With us something was wrong.

We sent no family portraits like those: I can't even find one. The closest we came were pictures of Tommy, a little boy with drooping hazel eyes, a sweet nose I loved to run my finger along, and a mouth full of cavities: a boy who bound us together. In pictures, Tommy is sun-drenched and giddy in blue trunks in a pool, clasped in happy Maggy's arms. He leans into me, sleepy, clutching Red Dog, or he sits in the garden beside his father, cross-legged in striped bell-bottoms. There's a single picture of Paul, Tommy, and me, a dreamy soft picture, we three close and open, but not one of us all together.

"Well, Paul just didn't take pictures," my mother has said. Yet each October when he's come to Germany for business, he always does two things: He solemnly hands me a card and check, because he visits just before my birthday and Jenny's, although he never visited her in Australia; and he always takes a picture of me. Near a wall, near a pumpkin, a single photo with whatever new little camera he's got.

"Go stand over there, Jane," he says, gesturing with his chin. I do. "This is the neatest damned camera," he says, "but I still haven't figured it out." He laughs, takes aim. And as I pose and smile near that pumpkin or wall, I always feel so flattered, so chosen and wrong in my alliance with those other girls' father, too much light spilling all over me.

———

My mother is right; Paul didn't take pictures of his new family, nothing like my father's portraits. Our half of the paper cut-out was too crumpled to compete. From the beginning, from the phone call between Washington and Canberra when Paul suggested my mother wait, failure had lurked. It could seep into the air at any moment, rising from something as small as the cat's pee puddle on the tasseled carpet. This tension had lived in each house, from the cold stone one on Connecticut onward. It walked hard up the concrete path and up the three brick steps, or through the sun-bleached white walls of Elsie's bungalow. If you looked at those houses you would say, But how delightful! Hard to imagine anything better than that courtyard house in Los Angeles: Lemon trees with sweet flowers grew by the windows, and a magnolia stood in the jungle out back, smelling of pencil, its unripe heavy blossoms furred, leaves brittle and glossy. I would love to have this house now. But only if it were mineral and vegetal, just those trees, that sunlight and stucco, no trace of anyone's thoughts or nights.

In that house: Paul and my mother had fought. Bitterly, about whatever they wanted. They fought about his mother and car trouble and the bloody Los Angeles freeways. They fought about Tommy's teeth and us. They fought about shoes and babysitters and beer. They fought about Karen Carpenter. And of course they fought about what felt like the main thing: that for Paul the whole damn thing had been a mistake, or my mother insisting he thought so.

The fights made the air unbreathable. Sometimes they were just words darting down halls and under doors. Often, too, doors and drawers slammed, my mother screamed, drops of blood were found on the floor the next morning. A ritual that began: Lying in bed with the light still on, I'd run my eyes without blinking along the lines between ceiling and walls, down each corner to the floor, along the baseboard — clear around the room without blinking, to make sure the room was sealed and safe. If not, it wasn't clear what would happen. The marriage would end, the house would break, Paul and whatever he meant would vanish.

Maggy and I shared a bedroom, and we'd lie in the dark, listening to it all crash at our door and hoping Tommy wouldn't wake up howling. If it was daytime, Maggy would march toward me with her lips tight and eyes fixed and whisper, "Let's just *go*." We'd put Tommy in his stroller, or each take a hand, and hurry over the freeway to a park. We'd push him in the swingset, we'd swing ourselves, our feet scooping out hollows in the sand; we'd take him by both hands and spin him until we collapsed dizzy on the grass; we'd lie on that tough grass and wait until the light had cooled and the fight might be over.

Then we'd walk home slowly, stopping to look at the cars rushing below on the freeway. The Mach IV was what the boys talked about at school, so I had a thing for the Mach IV, and I'd told Paul that's what I'd drive, as I'd told him I'd be a skydiver, as I'd do the Bruins cheer to make him laugh, and this was such a problem, this misalliance of mine, the way I did not avoid Paul like Maggy did, the way I'd silently decided to join him, win him, make him love me: Displace the real girl he'd lost.

Maggy and Tommy and I would stand on the overpass

and look through the chain-link fence at the cars whizzing by and far away at the yellow, vaporous horizon. Finally we'd have to go home. When we came into the courtyard, looked into the darkness through the doorway, stepped inside, the house would seem exhausted. Then our mother appeared in the dimness, a hand over her eyes, or sunglasses on in the dark, and there'd be a long loose drive on the pale Los Angeles roads as the sky turned orange, driving somewhere for fried chicken so we didn't have to be in that house.

Maggy and I would comfort Mom as she clutched and banged the steering wheel, until she'd toss her head free of tears and turn to us and say she was *fine,* everything would be just fine. After we'd bought our chicken and stood in the parking lot eating it from greasy wrappers or a bucket, we'd go near her and slip our arms around her waist, let her clasp us hot and close.

"My little mothers," she'd whisper. "What would I do without you." And the correct allegiance was clear.

But in 1970 Paul got a foreign posting in South America, and we were starting new. We all had the same name, or anyway wrote it on forms and it stuck. On the diplomatic passport I got before flying I signed *Jane Stuart Cummins,* "dependent of Paul Stuart." Maggy and I now sounded almost as American as he did, although our mother still had her South Australian lilt. She'd been obliged to give up her citizenship and be naturalized, and we were naturalized through her and gave up Australia, too. All American. And there was Tommy, little blond boy with dreamy eyes, binding us together.

The posting was Paul's first since Australia, our first since the United States, with our father. The girls wrote to tell us that new countries were exciting; our father wrote, *I certainly hope no-one tries to kidnap you! The ransom for two pretty girls like you would be high, so don't talk to strangers or go wandering off anywhere without asking!*

Eight days before we flew to our new post, the president there proclaimed himself dictator in an *autogolpe* and shut down Congress and the courts, and we landed during military rule. The land was as unstable as the nation: volcanoes, earthquakes, mudslides.

High in the Andes, it was a place of inky blue sky, baroque churches, new villas, limping dogs, the smell of shit and burning corn. We would live in a big yellow villa that stood in a garden of palms and hydrangeas and was fortressed by a stone wall studded with glass; to enter you pushed a button and waited for the electric gate to swing open. We weren't to be on the streets after dark; we weren't to go barefoot or swallow the water. Servants named Teresa, Miguel, and Cecilia lived in quarters out back, and Paul got a German shepherd we named Sultan, to protect us, a dog that was never trained and left bloody scratches down our legs, a dog that meant well but raged in the backyard and was finally shot by a soldier. The school we went to, Academia Cotopaxi, was also fortressed by walls, as white as the mountain the school was named for, and soldiers would ultimately march in there, too.

So many walls and compounds—the embassy as well, with its Marines and flag. Suddenly we were defined by contrast to where we were: Stuarts, Americans, gringos. Like a settler stepping into the antipodean sun, our name, culture, citizenship, and language were compacted within us, noticed only now that we'd arrived somewhere else. On the streets, we'd walk fair and green-eyed in our pale skins, belonging to another world, looking out at the new world around us. Women with black braids squatted beneath black hats, draped in heavy cloths the colors of parrots or flowers; little boys with brown rumps sprayed yellow pee in corners; old men with gnarled fingers and no feet, knees black and knotted, reached up from wagons. You walked past in the equatorial sun with whatever it was that lived inside your skin, all those American words.

Neighbors on Barnaby Street said to me later, when I was eleven, "You're very lucky to have done all that traveling. Most people never have the chance." Which was true. If you're the right age, you're not just placed somewhere foreign in a pot; you're film, and the light burns into you. *Identify* is a word that seems ruined, meaning to feel that you and what you regard are the same, and in South America I had instances of pure physical ecstasy, a transparency between myself and the natural world, as if the membrane lying between me and that splendor dissolved and we breathed each other.

The place was so brilliant, it could burn into anyone. Its steaming green ground, huge black moths like powdery bats, sky such indigo it seemed you could clutch it. Paul lifted me into the cool branches of a tree once to pluck an avocado, then showed me how to snap off the stem, poke it into the skin, and squeeze out pale green paste: paradise. You could drive to a monument at the equator and stand with one foot in the northern hemisphere and one in the southern, squint in that blinding yellow, blue light, and feel yourself on the globe, spinning. Paul took us to stay at a hacienda where Maggy and I rode horses, without rules and no idea how, just climbed on their warm, broad backs, pressed our heels into their flanks, and took off clinging into the wild, lush landscape, our mouths open as the wind whipped through us and we pounded through meadows along the sides of hills no one had ever stepped on. Maggy remembers this. It's one of about five things we remember the same, and when either of us mentions it, we both look away: away from each other but closer than ever, seeing and feeling that green rushing again.

I climbed Pichincha like Alexander von Humboldt and ran down a dune of sand and volcanic pebbles at the mountain's peak, seventeen thousand feet up in the air. Imagine being so high you see nothing but a mineral world, Andes peaks jagged and rising all around, peaks that at dawn are pink, pure sun upon pure snow and rock, while at night the stars take up more sky than the darkness and cast sharp shadows around your feet. Imagine being at the top of this, then screaming with so much pleasure it hurts and just running, rolling, down a sand dune in the sky.

So much consciousness suddenly. Do you wake up when you're nine? Before, maybe you had a mute understanding of your self as a glimmer of awareness in a body that moves and feels, but you're so embedded in this condition you can't express it. Then suddenly consciousness opens up with a shock. You are a physical, sensing thing in enormous place and time, all in motion. There's past, there's future, there's this unreeling *now*, the world is huge and heaving, there's so much *light*. At the same instant, you begin to understand the smallness of your self and the vastness of everything you *aren't*.

That consciousness should be contained in a body, in the hand resting on the branch of the Angel's Trumpet tree I'd climbed fast in the backyard to escape crazy Sultan, but that consciousness should not be in the branch itself: so strange, when dirty hand and branch looked alike, both mottled and dun, both cool, both bony. If I lifted that hand and drew it through the air, where it flew also flew consciousness — a swath of it pulled through the air — but then consciousness no longer was where it had been, resting on the bark. Why was it only inside a human or animal? Sultan barking down there, scratching the trunk, trying to reach my dangling foot — wherever he ran also ran consciousness; the air sparked with it behind him.

This strange conjunction of your self and all that's outside: The two meet at your eyes, your fingertips, your mouth as you swallow blue air. It was so stunning that physical senses, which were stuck in your skin, were exactly what let you fly *out* of your skin. But it seemed true. By looking hard you disappeared and became what you saw. Whatever you touched or looked at became part of you for as long as you touched or looked; for that moment you and it melted together. Lying on a hot lounge chair on the porch above that Angel's Trumpet tree, the porch off my mother and Paul's room, I would stare into the dizzying deep sky and feel myself dissolving into it.

————

But at that age, just as the world tears open around you, you also become aware of your own personal scope. I stood on the dining-room table as my mother took measurements for a uniform, and the numbers — twenty-two, twenty-two, twenty-two; fifty-four pounds; four-foot-ten — became a new part of identification: That was the shape and room I took up, and beyond it was the rest of the world.

Visible: dirty-blond hair, gapped teeth, green eyes. How to high jump, long jump, run the fifty-yard dash, cartwheel, round off, limber, back limber, play volleyball and soccer; how to hit the bull's-eye and win a gold medal. Because if you did these things right, medals showered like gold and adorned you. Accumulating little boyfriends — Gavin, Derek — was the same. They adhered to the skin, helped make you, their desire clinging and burnishing. I helped strip other girls at slumber parties and pretended to sleep while they stripped me, lying still under their appraising eyes. There was a curious shift in potency about this: The girl being stripped and stared at in the dark seemed more potent than the ones crouched around her, but whether it was our looking that made her potent or she possessed this potency on her own wasn't clear. She had something we needed to see. But if we didn't look at her? If we just shut our eyes? I kissed a girl in her closet, nibbled her baby breasts, touched her peach pudenda, and let her ponder mine. I kissed a boy under a blanket at a party, too, the crew-cut son of a huge Marine, and it was the clasp itself, being wanted, that meant everything: those hands and eyes, like medals, like gold stars.

In the blazing sun on a black square of asphalt I first saw

how a girl could have value, be a jar filled with gold coins. On a volleyball court in the Cotopaxi compound, the blue sky blazing and snowy mountains rearing all around, fourth-grade girls stood in gym shorts waiting to be picked for the team. One girl was picked, then another, and I suddenly saw with seasickness that for no visible reason, some girls had value and others didn't. Not value as players; that had nothing to do with it. Pure value, desirability. You could see it: Some girls were jewels, and others were nothing, they were trash, no one even looked at them. But the idea of value existed somewhere between the girl choosing and the one being chosen — who might have no quality beyond *being* chosen. So arbitrary, so magic. And perilous, too, because what could it mean if you didn't own that value but it was invested in you from outside? You only had it if someone else dropped her gold coin in you. Desire and desirability were a mingled current — the way when you looked at the sky, it was the current of *looking* that meant everything. Close your eyes, and girl or sky disappeared.

"I pick Desiree!" A girl who looked like Snow White, and Desiree was really her name.

"Then I get Susan!"

"I want Peggy!"

The captains' voices rang clear upon the hot black volleyball court with its invisible rules of rotation like the circlings of the planets, and those chosen girls, Desiree, Susan, smiled and walked in the sun to one side of the net or the other. The remaining girls waited, one drawn at a time, until only the worthless were left.

A strange economics, fluid and shifting. Maybe because this was the foreign service and a fresh influx of girls came every few months, we were replaceable, the currencies were liquid. Or maybe because we grew up in the air of politics and diplomacy, measuring worth was like breathing.

Or maybe if I were to find Desiree or Susan now they would say, We don't remember it that way at all. We didn't care about those things. But *you*: You had to win all the prizes, have all the boys love you, or you looked like you would actually die.

Another discovery at nine or ten: the peculiarity of our family. I told Peggy the story in a closet, the story of my doubled family, which I'd never told before. It had never seemed anything to tell, just the air around me.

There was silence. She looked at me in the dimness with eyes I've seen since, the troubled, defensive eyes of someone who does not recognize your language or species. I looked back at her in that closet, and suddenly felt I was looking out through the eyes of a hybrid, a griffin.

A last awareness, of position within the house, in Paul's eyes. Tommy was the baby, the boy, owned and adored. Maggy was discounted. But somehow I was like Tommy: favored, a blond pet with promise. Paul would glance upon me, eyes warming as he speculated what I'd become, as if I were actually his.

I've studied girls with real fathers since, and seen in those girls' eyes a look of absolute safety, as if they know they can tilt their heads back, close their eyes, and fall, and they'll be caught and nested, unconditionally.

Paul was not like that. He did not hand out love for free. And I'm glad for having had to earn it, because at least that meant not ending up with nothing. He was a star at the embassy, I've been told, and he preferred stars himself. He would look hard and keen at the world — local political tensions, the best convertible to buy, the new girls arrayed on the brown and gold carpet; he would look out measuring, judging. In each situation was a winner and a loser, and the winner he'd reward with the glow of the sun. My report cards, the bull's-eye I hit in a citywide meet, the boy under the blanket: These amused him. He'd look at me and smile, turn his warm attention on me — the best way to make clear who deserves favor is by cutting out the rest.

I was too smart, he would say to my mother, to become a teacher like her. And it certainly was good, he would say, that I wasn't developing as fast as Maggy, because then all that blood would drop from my brain. And I sure was one crackerjack student, he said, and look at those terrific drawings I did. I lay on the tasseled carpet and felt his rare gold sift upon me, felt it melting on my skin, until it became my skin, burnishing, stunning. And the faint, fine sense of being favored was an element of the high air in that house, nine thousand feet up in the Andes, air that was too thin, made you giddy. Maggy and my mother would nod to this now without saying a word.

But then the diplomatic pouch would arrive bearing those letters from the other side of the globe. *I don't know about these*

funny new schools you are all going to, whether you are really learn-
ing anything, and if so what. With the pictures tucked inside,
these letters fell in the stomach, disorienting, because it was
so easy to forget that other family, those other girls who had
displaced you. After reading the distant blue lines, you might
put out your hand to touch the sheepskin rug or the little
birds painted on the wooden chest and find that they were
no longer real, where you were was not real, what was real lay
on the other side of the globe.

But after a moment, with effort, those things could grow
solid. There was your bony ankle and the gold medal hanging from a red ribbon on the mirror, and if you sat still you
could hear Paul in his study whistling arabesques. And you
could fold that letter back up, run the side of your hand
along the edge, slip it back in its envelope, and tuck that envelope in the bag labeled *Daddy,* because he was the one not
really there, he was the one who had been replaced.

But. The way it had been in those other houses was how it
would be here. Such a beautiful house, gleaming wood floors
and the blue sky and mountains burning through the window's iron bars. But then the air changed; you could feel it.
The rooms were far apart, so it was possible to drift away
and shut out the fighting. Maggy glided to her room and
closed the door to concentrate on her candles and American teen magazines; I went to my room, where I'd crouch on
the porch and mouth a cigarette, or draw greeting cards, or
study Maggy's booklets about tampons. I wore hiking boots
and orange hot pants, made wings out of plywood to fly off

the back porch. In our rooms we could be busy and not talk about the fighting, or the girls, or where home was, or Paul, or our invisible father.

But when things reached a pitch, even in that big colonial villa you'd feel the heavy front door slam, the gate screech open, Paul's car jet off. A relief and a sense of disaster at once. In the silence Maggy and I knew that we had to do something. We probably sat on the floor or bed, wishing we could just be asleep, not know. But after a moment we'd get up, open our doors, look at each other across the dark hallway, move quietly together downstairs. We'd find our mother in the living room in the big gold chair, crying, a glass of wine in her hand. She'd look up and shut her wet eyes, fling out her arms, and we'd go to her, Maggy then kneeling on the floor by her legs, me hunched sideways in her lap, as she clutched her little miserable mothers, and we whispered whatever soothing words girls of nine and twelve can whisper about ruined marriage, until she fell asleep. Then we'd disentangle ourselves, arrange a blanket upon her, turn off the light, and run back up to our rooms.

And at some point Maggy would whisper in the dark, so hotly I could almost see her burning green and blue eyes: She hated Paul, and I should, too.

But once, when we walked down a hill, he held my hand.

An amazing sensation, almost holy, like a shark gliding toward you and not ripping off your leg but letting you pet his harsh hide. He looked down at me with his face utterly tender, the sky huge behind him, and offered me his hand.

———

The first June in South America we went to the beach for vacation. When you drive down mountain roads to the coast, you pass through the temperate zone to the torrid, a salty, glaring landscape of marshes and sugarcane. We reached the beach late at night, the flames from oil derricks dancing orange in the black. The Hotel Ensenada faced the ocean and was bleak, the days heavy and dull; June was not the season at the equator. We walked on the dingy beach, we went shopping at Libertad. I wrote in my diary, *Saw 2 sharks!* although they were just dogfish washed up on the dirty sand, but I saw fins everywhere and couldn't go in the water without picturing something gliding toward me, then panicking and bolting out. The sky and the water were swollen, gray. Except for the weekends, when Paul came down. Then the sky would clear to blue, and the beach became a real beach, golden. Paul brought the sun with him, my mother said; she'd shrug and laugh and say, "Here comes the Sun King," and although she doesn't remember this, I do, because with him there the sun shone on me, too. Swimming lessons: being held by him in that perilous water, rising with him in a wave.

At night we drove down the coast to Punta Carnero, a high promontory with a fancy hotel overlooking the Pacific. Marlins and swordfish hung on the walls, slot machines flashed in the game room, and from a pool on the cliff's high terrace you could swim gazing out at the wild, unswimmable ocean. Once we knew that June wasn't the season, the next time we went to the coast was January, and we flew down and took a cab to Punta Carnero, the driver swerving on the coastal road to avoid iguanas. The sun burned directly overhead, and Maggy, Tommy, and I spent our time in that pool or playing the slot machines, either out in the brilliance or manic in the dark. We got so burnt that at night Maggy and I peeled clinging strips of skin from each other's shoulders, and I'd take a strip and hold it up to the lamplight to see the networks of lines, then wad it like cellophane and ping it over at Maggy. The new skin underneath burned, too, and I still have a constellation of freckles on my shoulder from that equatorial sky.

One day, out by the pool, a cube of clear blue in a cliff, I put Tommy on a raft in the shallow end and climbed on beside him. The sun was so blinding, so hot on our faces and shoulders and backs, the water so cool. Tommy's hair was bleached by the sun, his laughing eyes tilting and hapless as he clutched the wet edge of the raft. He was three. I kicked us out, wobbling and splashing, toward the deep end, toward the edge of the cliff. An arc of blue sky, an arc of blue sea, the pool blue and rippling around us. We floated.

But something happened, and all at once I was underwater, spinning in the bubbles and quiet. Then the bubbles cleared and I saw Tommy. He had settled on the pool floor and sat there, plump legs before him, blond hair floating, head tilted as he smiled up at me. He didn't know water was different from air, that he'd drown. Yet I couldn't reach him, couldn't move through that water. He sat on the bottom and I floated, helpless, as light rippled upon him. Then suddenly there was a rupture in this serene world, a torrent of bubbles streamed down, and a long dark figure dove toward Tommy. He smiled and put out his arms to his father, who gripped him, turned, kicked off from the floor. And what I can't remember for sure is whether, in the moment Paul held

Tommy safe, he turned and looked at me through the water, those dark eyes stared hard and judging at me, as I floated there, useless, letting his son drown.

And really to tell the truth, I can't be sure if it was even me, or Maggy. If she was the one who put our brother on a raft and kicked out, lost her balance, let him tumble in; if she was the one to whom Paul turned with those condemning eyes before he kicked and shot upward. But it may as well have been me as her. It may as well have been both of us, two girls floating useless in the water, two girls who had never been Paul's real daughters, and certainly not his son.

The following summer we went on leave back to the United States, but Paul didn't come. When we flew, Hurricane Agnes had just begun gathering in the Gulf, revolving north. We stayed with Foreign Service friends, first in the suburbs of Virginia, which Agnes turned into thrashing green trees, falling branches, floating cars, gray shopping centers with boarded windows. When Agnes weakened we moved on, staying now with friends in an apartment downtown, a compound of curving white buildings. An elegant place with glass doors sliding open to curving white balconies like rows of teeth, and because the building curved, too, you could lean out over a toothed edge and see the building curve away around, or look out across to another white building with the same rows of teeth, or down to the blue, curving pool. The building across from us housed not apartments but offices. And the night we landed in Washington, five "plumbers" had broken into one of them.

While we stayed in the Watergate, swimming and racing the elevators and looking at fancy boutiques in the arcade, there was another break-in, a minor one, at home. I don't think I was told the details at the time, but later the story was this: Burglars climbed over our glass-spiked wall and up to the balcony off my mother and Paul's room, the terra-cotta balcony where I'd imagined dissolving into the sky, and from which I wanted to fly with plywood wings. The burglars dragged one of the chaise longues with its sharp metal legs to the edge and maneuvered it down to the garden. But to do this they made so much noise they woke Miguel. He ran out, and they fled with the chair.

The problem wasn't that a lounge chair was gone or that it had left scratches on the terra-cotta tiles; the problem was that those scratches formed a silent record of how searingly loud the theft had been. Yet in the middle of the night, only Miguel had heard. Paul hadn't, though the bed stood by the porch door. He hadn't because he was across town with his other woman.

My mother learned this when we returned, and by October Paul was gone. Apparently he left with only a suitcase. When we began packing the rest of his things—his leather table, cold, heavy whale's tooth, the tiger taken down from the wall—I asked Maggy what was happening. She was thirteen. She said, "Don't you know?"

I think Paul came into my bedroom to say good-bye, but now I don't know, I might have invented this, I might have decided he had to. I see the crack of light around my shut door widen, then his tall form hesitating, dark with light streaming around him. I think he comes in, sits uncomfortable at the edge of my bed, kisses my forehead, and whispers, "Well, so long, Pookala." But I know he left a present because I still have it, a fine silver pin in the shape of a llama, as it was nearly my birthday.

Just before the explosions, there'd been an evening when he called me into his study. It faced the garden of deep, soft grass where I'd turn so many cartwheels I could almost see the circles my fingers and toes had drawn like light in the air, and I'd stand still, dizzy, and look through the bars to his den. He had a teak desk and a shortwave radio he'd listen to with his head held close, eyes fixed hard on whatever he heard, the Bruins or a conversation about oil. The radio was heavy and smelled of steel and its worn leather case, and he'd shown me how to work it, twirling a pair of knobs until raw sound crackled to voice. A canary had flown in through the barred windows of that study, and this was the kind of thing that seemed to happen to Paul, as the sun came out for him at the beach, as he was a star at the embassy, the Sun King.

That evening before the explosions, he asked me to come in and shut the door. I did. He pulled a bag from a bookcase—he likes buying good things; a satisfied look turns his face tender when he ponders a fine carving or solid device. He turns it around in his hands, admires it, his eyes lost in appreciation. That evening he pulled a bag down from his shelf, drew from it an object wrapped in tissue. I don't remember what it was, an embroidered dress or a bread-dough figure, maybe. He unwrapped it, held it up, asked what I thought. I considered it, said it was really nice. He looked pleased and wrapped it back in its tissue, put it in the bag, returned it to the shelf. He just wanted to see if a girl like me liked it, he said, before sending it to Jenny for her birthday.

I don't even remember what the thing was, so I didn't covet it, wasn't envious. When I left his study I had a feel of honor, because I'd advised him on the matter of his daughter. Which was surely a position better than being a daughter, because it had not been born into, worth nothing, but won.

The silver llama Paul left me in a small leather pouch is the same size and delicacy as the silver peacock my father once sent from Asia, one of those fabulous gifts, so these two animals could be paired on the dresser or on a red velvet shelf of my bar-of-gold jewelry box. They won't face each other, though; their tiny silver feet and heads face the same direction, two animals heading west. Still, they could be paired like the tiny emu and kangaroo in the Australian seal on my father's letters, or like the emu and ostrich that parallel each other on their own continents, or like Paul and Daddy, or like Jenny and me, like the two shadow families had always been, except now with Paul gone the symmetry was broken.

Along with the silver llama pin, Paul left a note tucked in a very small envelope. It's written on one of his and my mother's engraved cards, on which he's crossed *Mr. and Mrs.* out. *Happy Birthday Jane.* He would be our agent for anything we needed from the United States, he said. *Love Paul.* I picture him in his study, at the teak desk, sipping scotch and fiddling with a pen and trying to figure out what the hell to write.

He's left-handed, and his writing does not slant forward in steady waves like my father's, but is backward, squashed, in jagged points and loops, extreme.

There was a day when Maggy and I packed our toothbrushes and nightgowns in plastic bags and took them with us on the Number Seven bus to school, but rode the Number Six home to a different house, as the one we'd lived in was too expensive without Paul, our only reason for being in the country. The new house was smaller, modern, white, and angular. It stood high in the hills overlooking the city, beside an empty paddock, fitting the slant of the hill. Square white porches stuck out all over, and you could climb from one to another to the roof. There you could sit and look out at the city and Pichincha with its single white peak I'd once run down, a mountain that had shaken one night since but not enough to do damage, and up at the inky blue sky into which smoke from the cornfields drifted, into which it still should be possible with enough will to dissolve, and you could throw one stone after another into the paddock, one stone fast and hard after another, trying to hit what you wanted.

That last year the diplomatic pouch had a new purpose: Now we could write letters to Daddy and Paul. Maggy might not have, but I did and recorded each in my diary. On February 25th I wrote to Daddy; on the 26th I wrote to Paul. On March 24th I wrote to Daddy; on the 25th, to Paul. In March there's also an entry that says, *I have a problem. I seem to be two people . . . and one is a plastic doll.*

Something else began to happen: I started to disappear. Or not disappear, just drift away. Like the glassy dream feeling when we'd first landed in Washington. I'd be walking with my mother down some brilliant, filthy street with its rich, warm stink of shit and smoke, and suddenly I'd be floating above us.

"I'm not here," I'd say.

She'd smile, squeeze my hand. "Of course you are, Janie. What do you mean?"

But I seemed to drift off, could not feel myself there, and even waving my hand before my face didn't make either me or the world real. It was disconcerting but numbing, oddly peaceful, slipping out of self.

We stayed that last year because Paul's post was supposed to have lasted until then, Maggy and I were still in school, and our mother was still teaching. Also because it wasn't clear where we could go, now that we'd given up Australian citizenship (cousins wrote, *You must be very disappointed that you shall never come back to Australia*). The ambassador liked my mother, couldn't have her abandoned on post, and arranged to fly us back to Washington at the end of the school year. He's the one who had first hinted what was up, she's told me: At a cocktail party he said, "Higamous, hogamous, woman's monogamous. Hogamous, higamous, man is polygamous."

A few months before Paul left the country, the president, out of favor with the U.S. government, was removed from office in a military coup. While we had been at Punta Carnero on New Year's 1972, the local commanding chief of the armed forces had made an official toast to the president and sworn the military's allegiance. But six weeks later, on Carnival Tuesday, that general deposed the president, and a military junta seized power. It was a school day, although during Carnival life was suspended and colored water balloons spun through the air. Soldiers marched through Cotopaxi's gates, and we were told to board our buses and return to our houses, because again there was military rule.

I wrote a novel based on this year, with a character who had a position like Paul's, and when the book appeared he didn't speak to me for months. Then suddenly he was back in touch. When I saw him on his next trip to Germany, he gave me a declassified State Department aerogram he had written at the time. "So you can see," he said, smiling and cocking his head, "what was *really* going on then."

No single group or likely combination of groups is currently able to pose a major challenge to the government so long as the armed forces give the regime their support . . .

In a black way I like to think that Paul was involved in the coup ousting the president, and that once he'd done his job he could leave — and had better. Just as I like to think that he had done this earlier, in Peru, where he once told me he was *persona non grata.* I even like to think that he was CIA. Recently I Googled him and got several hits that seemed to link him to the CIA, but when I ran the same search the next day to make notes, I got nothing. My mother says, "Oh, you romanticize him."

I don't have a letter from my father mentioning the fresh split, but just before we left South America for Washington he wrote a letter full of exclamation marks to say he'd been posted to New York and that we could come and stay very often in an apartment by Central Park. *I'm also writing to Paul tonight to tell him about Patricia and Jenny coming. I wonder what Nicholas will make of it all? . . . Helen and I are both very excited at the thought of seeing you. With love, Daddy.*

I'd like to think that I spent long nights in bed wondering about Jenny, Patricia, Nicholas, and Helen, but I didn't; they had occupied an aerial place for so long they couldn't come into focus. And the prospect of seeing my father: It fell into that congested black hole in my ribs where he'd lived for seven years, a place even more congested now because Paul had slid in there, too. But, anyway, the new political reality was clear: Now we'd been left twice.

In Washington the water had swirled down the drain the opposite direction from the water in Canberra. In Los Angeles water had sprung unannounced from sprockets hidden in the grass, sprockets that were fascinating to Maggy and me when we found them, like keyholes to an underworld; more fascinating when Maggy ran barefoot and a sprocket tore open her toe. On this posting the water was not to be drunk. It was full of life, unwelcome life you did not want clinging to the tissues of your mouth or swimming in your soft pink tubes.

The other thing you were not to do was walk barefoot. But to do cartwheels and handstands in the garden you had to, and maybe that's how I got a plantar's wart. It began as a small, flat disk on the ball of my foot, with a tiny hole at its center. I didn't feel it unless I stepped on a pebble that poked it; then the pain was exquisite and I'd lurch to the ground. The wart had dug deep into the skin. It took several years to learn what it was, and several more to kill it, by painting acid on the disk each morning, letting the acid burn through the top layer, then digging the flabby dead skin out, until finally the wart had been excavated.

I'd first discovered this hole in the Watergate. Sitting in one of the elegant bedrooms, I twisted my dirty foot around and finally found this tiny spot of intense sensitivity that made me buckle, as if my arms and legs hung on a string. This tiny hole that had so much power, but that I could ignore unless the right point pierced it. This was what the whole thing, the split, was like: a fine hole of weakness that ran through me, forgettable, buried, until touched precisely, then undoing.

4

Whenever I take the train from Washington to New York I try to feel again how it was in 1973, when Maggy and I first went to meet our father. But it's like trying to reconstruct your brain before reading trained your eyes to move left to right, before language honeycombed liquid life into cells of meaning: an ignorance that's unreclaimable. Sumac flies by, rail ties, corrugated sheds, shining water, numbers stenciled on posts. When we first rode that train, Maggy was fourteen, I was eleven, and speeding with us like our ghosts in the window was the sense that what had existed only in the mind for so long in fact lived two hundred minutes and miles away: Time and motion could work an appalling transfiguration. Our father would suddenly be real and seen, and so would we. To be exposed as well was whatever idea about love had lodged in my ribs, a fetal vision of what he'd think of me. If I'd been older it might have felt like a Presentation of the Virgin, climbing stairs and offering up self, virtues hoarded in a thin, amphibious body.

None of this was thought in words on the Amtrak that August; still it colored the blood in the veins. Seconds raced along the gleaming tracks, and soon just a hundred minutes remained, and how could only time and space exist between the imagined and the real? The two don't dwell on a continuum; between is only a leap.

When I was older, of sex age, a similar problem came up with men. To know a man by sight and conversation kept him abstract, a compound of image and language. He didn't yet exist in a way that could be felt or hurt. But if he wanted to touch or kiss or fuck me, the slide from abstraction to body was too much. I'd know it was coming and would panic, would picture his face growing closer, eyes and nostrils swelling like a cyclops, until it all blurred and his wet mouth swallowed mine. To get over this and manage sex, I'd drink and black out, wake up when it was over, and after doing that a few times I could face him. But this was later. In 1973 the problem was waiting for my father, who was only written words and pictures, to become a living thing.

Maggy says, "The problem is that you were too young when Daddy left to believe he still existed, even if you couldn't see him. To me he was always still there, and loved me."

We wouldn't see him as soon as we flew back to Washington in June, though, not until August. Between were months of drifting, trying to settle in a new place, new time zone, new hemisphere, new air, making your self all over again, starting over from watery nothing. It was Washington, not a new world, but this was the first time we were *alone,* as my mother said: just us, without a man. The goal was to make ourselves home in a place to which we were attached only by way of departed men who'd once given us names and citizenships — although the first name was gone and the second was not official, and my mother had burned her naturalization certificate in South America one night. Still, there was nowhere else to go. We landed at Dulles and began to start over, in a hot summer screaming with cicadas that's documented in my gold diary like a settler's experience in a strange new land.

My mother arranged to rent the old house on Barnaby Street, unbelievably available and cheap but not empty until the middle of July. Until then we'd stay with different Foreign Service friends. The O'Donnells had us first at their house in a new Fairfax neighborhood of pale cul-de-sacs, freshly poured curbs, and unfenced backyards that were a single green haze. It was broiling, the sky a dim gray blue. We rode bikes through the glaring streets to the drugstore for stationery and candy bars, staggered after the Good Humor truck when it rolled by in the shimmer, wondered how things would turn out, and worried.

My mother began starting over at once, driving the O'Donnells' car around the Beltway to look at used cars and interview for jobs. She applied to be a doctor's assistant (*but the agency says she's too good*), and to be a teacher again (*Sidwell Friends School liked her a lot, but right now they're all full. Mom hopes some teacher gets pregnant or quits*). She bought a car, very big news in my diary, but it failed inspection in D.C., so she had to drive it back out to be fixed and then drive it in to town again, and that time it passed (*got a license plate and every-thing. It's all okay! Now all we need is for Mom to get a job!!*). Mean-while we fought with and babysat the O'Donnell kids, wrote letters, rode bikes listlessly around in the heat, and did a lot of baking and mopping. The Watergate hearings droned and flickered in dark rooms. Maggy wasn't getting over jet lag, she was as limp as the blanched leaves outside, and when Paul called my mother because he wanted Tommy I'd hand the phone straight over and feel like a ghost, and June fell into July, and it wasn't clear if she'd get a job or where we'd go to school, and everything—the curving pale streets, the thin saplings stranded in the yellow front lawns—seemed bleached and exhausting. In the middle of this, our father called. I suppose now that this formed a helpful point on the imaginary continuum from written word to body, but then it just seemed blinding.

Maggy picked up the phone in a bedroom, and I picked up in the kitchen. I stood barefoot on the linoleum floor and stared out at the green haze, the receiver in both hands, Maggy's voice loud and breathy, too near. My diary says that my father's voice wasn't what I'd expected after seven years, although it doesn't say what I had expected, or that I'd ex-pected anything at all.

He said something like "How are you, chaps?" and when we answered, "Fine," he said, "My god, listen to those dread-ful American accents!"

To which we said, "Talk about accents—what about yours!"

I don't know what we talked about then, whether he made reference to the latest failed marriage; we got to business fast. How and when we wanted to come to New York, how long we wanted to stay. We were to write him on July tenth with our answers.

But Maggy became weaker and paler, soon had a temperature of 102, and was diagnosed with mono that would become hepatitis. So we packed up at the O'Donnells' and took her to Sibley Memorial, then checked into the Chevy Chase Holiday Inn, which seemed a step up to Tommy and me because there was a pool. We shared a single room that was dark, dark blue, the curtains pulled close against the glare; we kept milk, cheese, and orange juice chilled on the air conditioner to save money on restaurants. But we couldn't afford this and after a few days went to other friends, splitting up to make things easier, Tommy to one house while my mother and I went someplace else, then I joined Tommy while my mother went elsewhere. Meanwhile our furniture arrived and was being held somewhere, but many pieces were smashed. Maggy would stay in the hospital for ten days, after which she'd need to rest, and the trip to New York must be put off (*Or I go alone. Oh no*). All of this—the drifting, broken dining-room set, Maggy collapsing, us wandering apart, the failing cars, the mother with no husband or job but with a wrist she'd broken in South America that needed resetting, the awful absent presence of Daddy and Paul—infused these months with a weakness that seeped into the bones.

Housekeeping seemed to work against this, like a settler driving a fence around the place: warding off dissolution and chaos. It's not so easy to make yourself home. You know what it's like to wake up startled, not knowing where you are, until bit by bit the window and light shining in, the smudged wall, the scrap of paper on the floor become familiar again. Maybe you know, too, what it's like to wake up and, for a shocking moment, not remember *who* you are or what your name is, scramble in terror for a center; it's like being suddenly pulled out in the water and trying to touch down but finding no bottom, plunging under. Night blasts away identity and form. When I wake up, I feel dissolved, chaos spilling into the day, and I've got to get out of bed, get the sheets shaken and smoothed, reestablish order fast. Once the bed's made and clothes are put away, I feel better: nothing fallen apart yet. Maybe this struggle against dissolution is the soul of making your self home: a cell of order in streaming chaos.

At each of those places we stayed that summer I did housework — to earn my keep, make up for all that had gone wrong, I don't know; to pay for my alliance with the wrong father. At the O'Donnells' I cooked soup, baked brownies, mopped the linoleum; I designed hundreds of houses, pages of them in different colors, trying to get one right. At the next house I made muffins and polished the kitchen floor (*made everything bright and shiney*). I still vacuum and dust when I feel worthless or things are falling apart, because it's both productive and punishment.

Maggy finally emerged from Sibley in July, weak and spotted, and we moved to Barnaby Street. Around the house the shaggy fir trees drooped, their branches scraping the windows and telephone wires. The backyard stretched long and disheveled to an alley, with a clanking swingset, pocked raspberry shrubs, a stand of swaying oaks. But my mother kept making a new start, rising up each morning in her little flowered nightie, plunging like a divorced Mrs. Dalloway into each muggy day. She cut the lawn, pushing over and over it a rusted old mower that left limp, green strands for us to sweep from the sidewalk and stuff into bags. She clipped hedges, discovered ferns, shook out dead leaves from azaleas.

"Maggy! Jane! I need you, please!" Her voice lifted at the end, lifting up spirit; her face wet, bright, and tired; back straight.

We fell in. We swept stairs, cleaned windows sticky with pollen and cobwebs and June bugs, wiped sills whose paint flaked and chipped into the crumbling sponge. We mopped the linoleum kitchen floor opaque with layers of wax; we mopped the basement floor, too, cold black-and-brown tiles that stayed dull no matter how much Mop & Glo I squirted or how fiercely I rubbed, in a room that was large and dark, with a fireplace and a door that opened to the backyard, a basement full of potential but always hopeless and musty, until my mother finally rented it out to boarders, at least one of whom stole. We scoured brittle black-and-white shower tiles held together with rotting grout. I raked leaves, found nails and plugs to fix my broken desk, made an unsteady night table from a splintering tea chest, hemmed cutoffs, sewed felt animals to send to our grandmother Dora because it was important always to make things, to be productive as well as industrious, and kept distressed accounts of what anything cost (*SOUR MILK FOR 59 CENTS!*). We vacuumed the cream living-room rug with its trails of flying wine drops from all those glasses thrown in South America, Los Angeles, and this same house a stepfather ago. My mother went at the rug with a toothbrush one day. She had crouched to scrub a spot but moved on from there, finding one stain after another, crawling across it on reddened hands and knees as if retracing her life, spooling it back in, following the crumbs back to hope and potential, her days with bare legs and a blowing dress on a South Australian shore.

"Come on, girls!" she cried, looking up as we tried to creep past, drops of sweat running down her long nose. "Help me."

We wanted to read, watch television, eat ice cream, sleep, but we dropped to our knees, dipped toothbrushes in suds, and began scrubbing, heads down, resentful, eyes burning with tears. Only later, when she had stood stiffly and leaned in the front doorway through which Paul used to pass with his polished shoes and hard eyes, as she stood there gazing out at the August haze and the prospects of life with two marriages behind her, no job, far from home, only then did we glance at each other and whisper, "Why are we scrubbing a rug with a toothbrush? Is she crazy?"

But seeing her straight back as she stared out at the oaks, I knew I would fly at anyone else who said so, as if the attack were personal.

We only rented at Barnaby Street, didn't own it, but we would stay there for years, and it grew around us like a shell. Home economics: Maybe the most ancient form of economics is to hold a house around you, managing what goes in and out

— the stern spirit of Dora, who had saved the white-wash water for the colors and stitched from scraps that peacock robe. Little things my mother did that I learned to do, too, like saving each bit of string or pink rubber band that comes around the newspaper, keeping them in a drawer and not needing to buy such items, making everything count. Never throwing away an old, bruised banana but mashing it for muffins; folding the towels in halves, and halves again, and piling them warm with the rounded edges aligned, blue, yellow. Making sure there's enough milk and that it never goes sour; cooking our own paste from flour and water; using the leftover peas and carrots in meatloaf. Days and weeks like this, handling food and running a sponge over each surface of the kitchen, make you feel as if you're stroking the house itself. We had an old dishwasher that must be rolled to the sink, its tubes screwed into the faucet, before you turned the dial and the machine stirred to life. In the dark, the washer rumbling, I'd lay my head on it, press my cheek against its warmth, shut my eyes. My mother's old black Singer that ran with a foot pedal—the warm smell of machinery, thread, and cloth were so soothing as you bent over to guide a hem past the plunging needle. I got to know with my fingers the beveled edge of each wooden stair I swept with the soft, black hand broom, the grained oaken roundness of each bulb of the bannister, the worn hem of each tea towel and sheet. We grew into each other.

But the composite was tighter than that, synecdochal again. This house was a woman's, no man this time. The house would be a form of my mother, and not just her, but her little mothers: us. How she set the table was how we now did. If, weeping, she placed a glass of water between herself and the onion she chopped, we learned to do that, too. She'd suddenly start sponging the floor in the morning while still in her nightie, and although I hated this then, I do it today, and feel I'm actually her each time I crouch on the tiles and see my strong hands, my bony knees, like hers. Barnaby Street was where self, mother, and house merged, fathers and fatherlands gone. An organic compound and very female. Tommy, at five, stood before a mirror one evening, plucked the shirt from his chest, and asked when he would get bosoms, too. But his father came to fetch him on weekends, so even this slight chameleon boy left the house, left it entirely female. A humid female compound whose counterparts now were Paul's glassy apartment downtown and that real family's official residence in New York.

In the middle of all the sweeping and swishing of toilets, my mother went to the hospital to have the wrist she'd splintered in South America reset. While she was gone, Maggy and I made macaroni and cheese and kept mending, cleaning, arranging our rooms: the gold-bar jewelry chest, silver elephant, colored bread-dough figurines from South America; the medal for throwing set on the white dresser that once had been Paul and my mother's and now was mine; certificates pinned to the pale-green cork wall.

One night while she was in the hospital, the girls called — a new point on the nonexistent continuum, midway between that tape they'd sent four years earlier and their real breathing selves in New York. Daddy and Helen had gone out for the evening, so the girls were alone, like us. Unlike us, they'd discussed and imagined their stepsisters; we already existed in their minds. They'd surely planned, watched to see where Daddy kept his address book, waited until he and Helen had left, looked at each other, and nodded. One of those critical differences between us: To excavate a plan like this from the murk of the present was beyond us. I don't think we once pictured those girls, because we couldn't see farther than the window screen or stained porcelain sink. We were just trying to make the house run and hoping our mother got a job and maybe a boyfriend and that life would work out. We would never have dreamt, anyway, of calling long distance. *There'll be a large bill!* my diary frets. *They asked some pretty strange questions.*

What these were I don't know. The girls knew their father lived on the other side of Rock Creek Park, so maybe they asked about him. Maybe they asked about his girlfriend, who lived with him downtown. As I write this, though, I know it's wrong. They would never have admitted to something about their father we knew but they didn't. Instead they probably asked if we wore bras and when we'd started our periods, and I just sat there with the receiver burning my ear.

In August, Maggy and I finally went to New York. I'd laid out my clothes for the train trip like a flat mannequin on the other twin bed, to be as ready as possible. Our father had stressed the need to reach Union Station early, as if in all likelihood we would be late, because girls belonged to a species that always was late. Sure enough, either the car wouldn't start or my mother didn't know the way, so we rode the bus to Union Station, and as it kept stopping to let slow old people off or on, or turning and chugging in what seemed the wrong direction, and the time for our train got closer and the station was nowhere in sight and we didn't even know where it was, the idea of arriving too late made me nearly physically sick. But we got there, ran through the marble cavern beneath the stone Indians standing high on the cornice, found the right platform, and boarded. My mother waved her bandaged wrist as our train pulled out.

The air-conditioning had broken, my diary says, and the cars were 90°, but I remember only a vaporous sense of heading toward something that both took up no space and enveloped. Maggy and I gazed out the window at Baltimore's hot brick turrets and marble steps, played Alphabet, and lurched to the café car for M&M's. We found the paper cups in the dispenser and stared out the window again. Sumac, kudzu, old cracked tires, shimmering heat as we skimmed the shining rails toward our father.

It was the first time we'd been on a train since leaving Washington in 1965. Maggy had spent half her life with her father, half without; she sat quiet beside me. The subject of our family had sunk inside us to a private, dark zone so deep and compacted that the cold water there took different molecular form; no words would bubble up from this place. I looked out the window and thought elsewhere. A quarry, hills of gray pebbles, pink graffiti, the hot gleam of the track. I wondered whether a pen tossed up would keep moving at the same speed as the train or, touching nothing, would be freed from the motion and hover still like the landscape we rushed through, so I kept tossing my pen to find out. Vistas of water, Johnson & Johnson, blue plastic swimming pools, children looking up and waving gravely as we sped by like they knew where we went. The expectations you might have if you were conscious of your mind: anticipation of union, a true state restored.

Trenton. Through the thick scratched window, green suburbs started to give way to rusted cars and swamps filmed with scum. New York appeared on the horizon like a toy city, as if the towers would only reach to your hips and you could kick through them if you wanted. But as the swamps spread out the city grew large, the train shot into a tunnel, and this is when panic began, the secret about to be real. We slid into a slot of cool granite light, back into hot darkness, then stopped. Beside me Maggy snapped open a mirror.

We were to go straight up to the announcement board. We were not to talk to anyone or wander off, or we would never be found. He'd asked, to be safe, what we'd be wearing.

We pulled our bags from the rack and dragged them off the train to the sooty platform, up stairs crowded with hot pants and tall heels caked in glitter. In a dim middle layer we stopped, but it didn't seem right, so we went up another flight to a glare of hot dog stands, electronics, noise.

An announcement board hung above a crowd, and we lugged our bags over to stand beneath it. We waited. Hundreds of faces in the noise, and one might be his, and we searched each man about the right age. But no one looked enough like his picture, and everyone moved, and there is no continuum between image and moving life. We stood there, wondering if we'd gone to the wrong place or had come the wrong day, and how it could be we didn't know our own father, when suddenly a figure stepped from the crowd, and I wish to god I could remember the instant, but there was too much noise and motion, and what I remember most was that as he came toward us beside him walked a woman — and somehow, despite everything, I had forgotten about her.

I'm sure he embraced us, I'm sure he beamed, I'm sure the rusty word *Daddy* gurgled out of our throats. I'm sure Helen embraced us, too, and that we both looked down giddily at Nicholas, this other half brother for whom we'd carefully brought a present, *a little moving dog,* whatever that is. But I don't remember Nicholas being there or even quite grasping that he actually existed; I don't remember seeing my father then at all, as if the fantastic moment had finally come but exploded at once into a black hole. We probably chattered stupidly about the hot train as we rode up the escalator and climbed into, I think, a black Checker; if it wasn't a Checker that first time, it was the next, a cab converted to be my father's official car. Either that time or later he had a driver, and we sat all five in the back. I sat on the little fold-down seat, which I might have liked then because it was novel but it also made me ridiculous, knees jabbing my chest, a fossilized bird. My mouth and head had filled with air. Maggy and I looked out the windows, made the mistake of twisting and craning to see the tops of tall buildings, and Helen touched my father's hand and said, "Look, darling. Of course they've never seen skyscrapers."

We drove up to an apartment across from Central Park with a gray awning and top-hatted doorman, a deep gleaming lobby, and an elevator man who matched the doorman, slid shut the brass gate behind us, and cranked us upward. The gate slid open to a vestibule with a little table, a vase jetting flowers, a door affixed with the Australian seal. My emu and kangaroo, which suddenly belonged to a foreign world on which I had no claim and which, like my father, had now been sliced out of me, set free.

The apartment was elegant and long. That summer it was being redecorated, so walls were torn down and floors were torn up, but what I see is its serene, finished state. Large paintings of colors and shapes hung on the walls, doors opened upon other rooms with more paintings, flowers, boomerangs, spears, plush sofas, a glass table with small silver boxes. Overlooking the park was the master bedroom, where the royal bed seemed always made, smoothed with satin, silk pillows plumped. Into this my father and Helen would disappear, the door closing silent behind them. That very long, narrow hall, papered in photos, not as bamboo, as I insist on remembering, but as a garden trellis, led to the deep end of the apartment. A door on the left opened to one bedroom, and a door on the right opened to another just like it, except one was yellow and the other was pink; both smelled of shampoo, watermelon soap, fresh plastic. The pink room was Jenny's, and I would sleep there; Maggy would stay in the yellow room. Our first two days in New York the girls were in Washington with their father: that's how it had been arranged. The carpet was thick and absorbed sound.

In Jenny's room: a new radio and skis and her own bathroom, pink flowered wallpaper and bedspreads and a bedside table that wasn't patched together like mine. I probably tried not to touch anything. I mentioned none of it in the diary. I also wrote nothing about how she'd adorned her dresser and desk, stuck medals and ribbons from horse shows all over. Or about the pictures she'd displayed, the same as had been sent to us but taken a minute earlier or later in the sequence; and framed private pictures of her own personal Paul. Also not a word about the things she'd traveled with from the Middle East to Asia to Canberra to New York, things she'd recently unpacked and run her fingers over and looked at and were *hers.* Nothing about the silver elephant whose halves came apart in the hands, or the bar-of-gold jewelry box inlaid with arabesques and the name *Jennifer.* Or about the paper she'd left on her desk, where she'd printed hard: *Jenny Cummins. Jenny Stuart. Jenny the Greatest.*

In my diary I report that we unpacked, ate dinner, gave presents, and looked around Fifth Avenue, which seemed big and nice in the night. Nothing else. I went alone to Jenny's room, Maggy to Patricia's.

In the photos taken that summer, pictures in which we now magically figure alongside that poised family, the girls stand close in new matching flowered culottes and platform sandals, what New York girls wore that summer, but I'm in cutoffs of pants I'd had for three years. I'd scissored off the legs and hemmed them and sewn patches to the worn bottom ("Have a nice day!") — and this still seems proper; it's my mother in me, and her mother, too; my mother has her first colander from 1957. But patched things, unmatching things, in New York were noticed, as seemed to be the facts that Maggy and I hadn't brought much in our suitcases, and our swimsuits looked at least two years old, and we stared at the private bathrooms as well as the doorman and skyscrapers, so by our first morning, we were the poor girls come to visit. We were taken straight to Saks.

A treat, a spree, it should have been wonderful, yet it's one of those moments Maggy and I remember the same: grim. Giddy as starvelings after the sickly summer, we lunged among the mannequins and racks, while my father looked on, smiling, rocking back and forth on his heels. Jeans, spangled T-shirts: We clutched and gaped and fingered things, but Maggy couldn't make a choice because it must be the right one. Buying clothes was so rare it mattered; we were not used to gliding into stores and getting what we liked so easily. And I couldn't choose because suddenly, in a dressing room, trying on a glittery red T-shirt, my head began aching so much it seemed ready to crack, fossilized in the layers of the problem. If I put that shirt on and let them buy it, I'd be bought, too: Something important would have been surrendered. And to get anything so easily made it worthless: I wanted that glittery red shirt but could not have it given, not given by them. And beneath this was another problem, that to be newly clad and then eyed with approval meant that something had been wrong before. Whatever I lacked threaded back to my mother, the woman who had astonishingly not supplied us with our own face creams and lotions. The first thing he and Helen seem to have noticed: not even a part of me but of her.

This was a shock, for the first time recognizing my own self by contrast and finding it not my own making. In New York with my father and Helen I first became my mother's daughter, born of her flesh and drenched in her being and in the stories told about her. And in this household she was not welcome. Another thing my diary doesn't mention but I remember: In photo albums, she'd been cut out.

In the dressing room in the Girls' Department at Saks, a red shirt half tugged over my staticky head, I went rigid with pride and despair. When I finally came out I said I'd buy the shirt myself. I had just enough money. My father threw up his hands and laughed and dismissed me, I flushed and grew more black and mute, Maggy stood paralyzed among the racks, arms draped in jeans, worried that she'd squander the treat and angry at being teased for this worry, and my father and Helen had probably never seen such a performance, and we were not only the poor girls but absurd.

None of this appears in the diary, though, just a note about how nice D and H were and how Maggy got a pair of overalls, jeans, and two shirts and how much I liked the red shirt they bought me. Then how grand the Statue of Liberty was, and the Twin Towers, and the Met. My father is not mentioned beyond this; in those first two days his face never seems to detach from the shop windows on Fifth Avenue, the seats of the black Checker, or that other face, Helen's, always paired with his, her dreamy, knowing blue eyes always drawing away the light of his. I don't remember a minute alone with him. And after the second day, after lunch and looking at Chinatown and Wall Street, he left us with Helen and went to Penn Station to pick up the girls, and he does not appear in the diary again, as though he really did recede into a black hole, like Paul, his absence overwhelmingly present.

There would be many first times I saw Jenny: at the Girls' Grammar when we were four and five; now in New York; later, in Washington when she was seventeen; and in Sydney when I first flew back. Of these the only one I can see stark and clear is the last, Australian light streaming behind her when the door at Sydney International slid open. This time, in New York, when she first emerged whole from my father's glossy photos, I picture her pacing fast and soundless down that long hall that was or wasn't bamboo and finding me in her pink room, stopping dead in the doorway, out of breath and hot, letting one narrow hip jut against the jamb as she regards me. Or maybe Maggy and I waited in the vestibule for the brass elevator gates to slide open and the girls to step out, like the staff lined up to receive them. I know it was thought out, as every part of these visits had to be, and it was surely a task to have all these kids for two or three weeks while settling in a new city, among them two new girls who could pose problems. The first decision had probably been to make sure each pair of girls had two days undiluted with their own father. And now that those two were coming back, my father went alone to the station to meet them. Maybe because this made logical sense, or maybe to assure them that although we were there, he was still their Daddy — or maybe, who knows, to debrief them.

So Jenny either came striding down that bamboo hall and found me lurking, or we paced down it together, but when we were alone in her carpeted pink bedroom, one of the first things she said was, "It's terribly important to Daddy, you know, to treat all of us exactly the same."

Which must have been easy, given how alike we were. She was just an inch or two taller, her prettiness midway between doll-like and wicked, with wavy brown hair and quick brown eyes and just enough new little breasts to put in a bikini, and hip bones beginning to open. I was a year behind, with stringy, wavy blonde hair and the body of a boy. But we were both smarty star girls, thin, fast, and mortally competitive, and as we looked at each other there was no forgetting our birthdays or names. I see her, once we're alone in her room, being studiously nice, because I'm a guest, and Daddy's daughter, and Mum's stepdaughter, and Father's former stepdaughter, and Nicholas's half sister, and Tommy's half sister, and so a *sister*, after all, but eyeing me, seeing whether I'd been sleeping in the right bed, and whether I'd put my things in the right drawer, and what sort of things I'd brought, and how many, and what I'd put in her private bathroom. She didn't have to make clear that this pink room was hers, as were the apartment and New York and America — but then there was her father's in Washington, where she and Patricia had just been. They looked like they'd been trampolining high and fast, and this had won them a gunshot laugh but no more. Maybe Jenny had learned that her father, unlike mine, did not treat everyone exactly the same. Maybe she'd learned that he liked a good race and especially liked the winner.

So we'd race. We jostled in the car to Jungle Habitat, we raced bikes in Central Park, we competed at something called Make It, Wear It, Share It, where we did the first two but not the last. We jostled at Gimbels, where I bought washcloths for my mother; at the museum bookstore, where I bought bookmarks for my mother, and why the bloody hell, the girls said, did I think so much about my mother, did I have some sort of complex? Up and down hundreds of hot narrow stairs inside the Statue of Liberty (*Patricia said "Well, if* JANE *could make it* ANYONE *could!" She's never climbed a 17,000 foot mountain! P is getting me so mad it's pathetic*); at the planetarium (*It was really fun, how the world could end*); at Radio City Music Hall, where we saw the Rockettes and a movie called *Nightwatch* with so much stabbing I ran out hysterical as the girls howled with laughter; at a friend's pool: Everywhere, we jostled and raced.

At that pool, in a dappled leafy garden in some Cheever-esque suburb, Jenny discovered my weakness fast. She swam behind me underwater, then clutched my leg with sharp fingers like teeth so that I screamed and kicked, or she suddenly lunged from the water before me with her eyes dead and mouth drawn down like a shark, before hurling herself back into the water gasping with laughter while I splashed in panic to the steps. Safe on the grass, then, she and I stood hip to hip, Jenny in a bikini and me in the blue one piece I'd worn my whole life, hurling darts at a bull's-eye until we'd nearly hurled away our arms, to see who was better, more clever, more able, really worth something, really should win, in fact should be the *only* one there because we could not both exist. The diary never mentions either father.

I say what appears in that gold diary and what doesn't because of what this seems to show about consciousness and memory. You remember deeply a moment or the tone of a day, how it burned your skin or stabbed into your ribs. Yet at the time you say nothing, not even to yourself, so it exists without words and is like an animal dwelling mute in your tissues — the sort of memory that smell arouses. This layer of consciousness, a flash of image, a tearing sensation, settles deep beneath the ordinary things that are articulated at the time, and works itself to the surface only gradually, like lead paint burning through wallpaper. The battles with Jenny were comical because we didn't know what they meant — or I didn't, anyway. What lay buried and mute was the panic that after seven years my father seemed likely to slip out of reach while standing there, never closer. He might finally look at me but blink and see nothing. Or look at me but see only Jenny, or see only my mother, or hear not my voice but the America of Paul. And maybe the same had undone Jenny in Washington; we both *still* might not be visible. The only thing to do was slash in the water, find the other girl, and push her down.

So each night, once my father and Helen had closed their door safely at the far end of the hall, we struggled. In the yellow room beside us, the two older girls whispered and told things, I don't know what, their secretive S's floating under the door, and between Patricia and Maggy never would be what there was between Jenny and me, because between them was not that problem of Paul; between Patricia and me there wouldn't even be quite what there was with Jenny because we were too far apart and unlike, not mirrored, not fixed together night after night in twin beds.

In her pink room, Jenny and I struggled. We arm wrestled on the edge of a bed, our faces red and eyes popping, teeth bared and lips drawn back, juddering—but Jenny was just enough bigger to win, which enraged me. We could both do cartwheels and limbers and competed, obsessive, flinging our bodies in T-shirts again and again hard on the burning carpet. We were boy-girls, slim, hysterical muscles. We both had compulsive rituals and fought to see who was worse: Jenny had to stand at her bathroom door and smile and wink at the tub, the shower curtain, the toilet, the sink, before turning off the light, still smiling. I had to lie in bed and run my eyes, without blinking, along each edge of the room, each line where the ceiling met each wall, down to each corner, along the edges of the floor, and if I blinked once I had to start over.

"What the bloody *hell* are you doing!" Jenny said when she caught me. But I'd seen her at it, too, and ran to the bathroom and stood in the doorway and mimicked her smiling and blinking.

"It's neurotic, you know," she informed me, looking pleased. "Mum says I'm neurotic."

She pronounced it *nee-u-rho-tic,* with breath, and that

was the sort of thing that made clear she'd taken my country, too, she held it right in her mouth. She could just open her lips and I could see behind her white teeth my precious emu and kangaroo, now her own little pets, just as she could open her mouth and say sweetly, "Daddy," taking him and my word and accent at once. And in her, too, behind her lowered lashes, was that lost place of mine, which she'd seen and touched and breathed just before coming to New York — Australia was hers, so I had to throw it away and hate it. I had to mock her Australian accent, and she had to mock my American one, because she looked at me and my mouth and saw the corollary of what I saw, and we fought violently over how to spell *aluminum,* which she pronounced *aluminium,* and when she ran off into the bamboo and came back shaking a British dictionary that spelled it her way, I was utterly defeated.

Finally we were exhausted and collapsed on the twin beds. The radio played softly between us in the dark (*You used to say, Live and let live . . .*), distant sirens and car horns drifted in through the window, and for a sleepy moment we might have realized that we liked the same things, cartwheels and words and puzzles and insects, we were *alike,* maybe we liked each *other.* But then we remembered who we were, and that we could not afford this.

Maybe that first visit she said it, or maybe the next. There were so many nights like that, so often when we lingered on the verge of being just two girls, not creatures embedded in this doubled family. The darkness opened up around us, winging, and maybe it only does that for girls of eleven or twelve: Pan girls, slight, strong, and desirous. You lie still on your twin bed and can barely keep from breathing your self out into that darkness in excitement and yearning. We lay side by side, a narrow, carpeted moat between us, those songs of 1973 blooming in the darkness, bearing us up, like floating. So much of your own passion is locked in old songs, they're as powerful as scents, and when you hear them again they slip into your blood and imbue it again with the color and tang of all you so badly craved in those years, even if you couldn't name it. We shut our eyes or gazed at the shadowy ceiling and sang or dreamed along. On my side was the open window, sounds of the city filtering in and blending in the air above me — the currents of nighttime city and song tugging outward, exciting, so that I lay on that bed like on a raft, life pulling me. I had that window opening to air; but on Jenny's side was the door to the long bamboo corridor leading to the master bedroom, our paired parents, the chambered heart.

So one night, on this visit or the next, Jenny said the thing that had moved through her mind and would now infect mine. I don't think she even turned toward me, just gazed up at the ceiling in the darkness, perhaps stretched a bare leg into the air, and whispered:

"Who do you think did it first?"

I probably flipped over in bed and refused to answer, smashing the pillow around my ears while she laughed and speculated singsong to the ceiling. But her question sank like a chunk of pigment and slowly infused my blood: It couldn't be thought about yet, but colored everything. She surely needed her mother to have done it first, to have chosen and won what she wanted; otherwise Paul had, and therefore had wanted to leave her mother and been able to leave Jenny, too. And I'd need my mother to have done it first, because otherwise my father had and had easily left me. For my mother to have done it first, Jenny's father must have. For one of us to get what she needed, the other had to lose.

To be or not to be wanted: the only measure of value.

By the second day of that visit, something had overtaken me when I was near my father, and it would overtake me again and overtakes me still. A stupidity, a dullness that made me stare at the ground. My mind went flat; I could say nothing worth hearing. (*Stop staring at the ground, Jane! Will you stop grimacing at the camera, please!*)

On outings, my father appointed the time for us to be bathed, dressed, and ready at the door, and he told us the order in which we should climb into or out of the car, the order in which we should sit. We were not to jostle. We were called *You lot. Will you lot be quiet back there!* We were lined up for pictures on bicycles, or before a pond in Central Park, or on the Staten Island ferry. When not driving or lining us up, he kept at a safe, cheery distance, jingling the coins in his pockets, never quite catching my eye, smiling but glancing at his watch, then looking around for where his wife might have got to, hurrying off to her when she appeared.

And she: She was beautiful and composed, crisp lace glimpsed beneath a blouse, smooth legs, tasteful sandals. She could cast her blue eyes this way or that, and everyone would watch. She was like Madame Merle; she knew things.

Artists, books, philosophers, ideas. Hadn't we read that yet? Didn't we know? Degas, Diderot, Jasper Johns. Had I seen their work? Surely I'd *heard* of them? I was eleven and had heard of nothing. Her speech fell like a waterfall sparkling with names, names you were just trying to spell in your mind when out danced the next one, and beneath this shower I'd grow sullen and stupid, bitterly resolving to learn. Was that really how we'd been taught to set a table? Could it be true our mother didn't buy us our own creams? Never mind: Helen would buy them herself. She took us to the Met and Frick and Guggenheim, she pointed out details in an Ingres sleeve or a shade of blue, she taught me how to etch and print, she bought us Napoleons and éclairs in cafés, and my mother did not do such things, my mother did not know such things, my mother did not hold on to husbands, and thinking those things — as I watched Helen glide through a door held open by a top-hatted doorman and step out onto sunny Fifth Avenue, and as I pictured my mother scrubbing a rug with a toothbrush — I felt sick with betrayal. Because I knew which woman I loved and was *better*. But I could see which woman I would rather be. My father's eyes lay always happy upon her; between them ran a silvery leash. And witnessing this — from a low position, through cracks in a cave, a Gollum position — seeing a woman who possessed a value that drew to her what she desired, a woman who alone was gold: It was like seeing the mystery itself.

When the two weeks were over, we said good-bye to Nicholas and the girls (*I'm not heartbroken about leaving J + P*) and stepped with our bags through the sliding brass gate, rode the elevator, got into the black car. Helen might have sat in the front seat this time and talked to the driver, while we sat in the back with Daddy between us, the kind of fair thing he would have planned, giving our arms a squeeze now and then and glancing at each of us brightly, looking hopeful; otherwise the three of us gazed at the large windows of mannequins in gold dresses and furs rolling by.

"Did you remember," he whispered, "to thank Helen?"

We reached the station and took the escalator down, down again to where the trains waited in the darkness and heat.

"It was wonderful to see you both," Helen said on the platform, and kissed us. "Please give my regards to your mother."

"Thank you," we said. "For everything."

We found a pair of empty seats, and our father swung up the luggage and gave Maggy the tickets. He stood with his hands in pockets, jingled coins, and glanced up the aisles, back at us, smiled, glanced away again. The train jolted.

"Uh-oh," he said. "Time! It was wonderful. Call, hmm? Write? Don't look so glum! Soon you'll be up again." He kissed us both, made sure our bags were in order again, and hurried off. We saw him out on the dark platform then, peering through the train's tinted windows, and pounded on the glass until he saw us and threw up his hands as though it were all new.

The train wasn't moving yet, so we pressed against the window, and he looked up and down the tracks, made I-don't-know expressions, shrugged. He wrote with his finger on the window, backward: *c–u soon! xxxooo.*

Finally the train jolted again and inched forward, and he mimed surprise, alarm. He walked alongside us, and as the train gathered speed he jogged athletically, lifting his knees and elbows high. But then we were really moving. He gave up, smiled, made a boo-hoo face, wiped his eyes, and waved.

Riding silently through the tunnel and out among the belching machinery of New Jersey, I felt a weakness, a loosening near my ribs, as though a plug had been pulled and something were spiraling out, something essential, like blood.

I didn't know what I'd wanted on that trip to New York. Maybe that a long sleep would be over, I'd wake to see my father smiling through the airplane hatch. He would finally *see* me, and I'd be restored. I was a hero who had been mistakenly exchanged and had tramped the earth and proved himself and now at last would be recognized.

Maybe all four girls had boarded their Amtraks with the same occult craving, too much to commit to words, to air. Maybe, alone in our beds the night before we took our trains north or south, a private image of an ancient lost union with our fathers had risen in each of our minds. Then, later, maybe each got back on the train stunned — and when we first saw the girls, as always, they were a step ahead, they'd already seen their father and learned what they learned while we were still beginning. Maybe we sat on an Amtrak rattling through Delaware, staring out the window, not sure what had happened but realizing already that our fathers could be lost again, we'd fail again to make them love us.

———

But still. Still, I can picture other things that might have happened on that first visit, little events to balance the last day we'd seen our father, seven eerie years earlier. We might have gone for a walk around Central Park, just Daddy and Maggy and me, arm in arm, and he might have said, Listen, let me tell you about those years, let me hear how you *were*.

This didn't happen, and I'm glad. To have such tender regard and concern for health would ruin this story and turn it to sponge. I prefer the silence and pounding on glass.

5

Layers of consciousness seem like zones of ocean water, dropping from a surface that's glittering, warm, salty, and blue, to cool green volumes shafted with light, down to cold currents that roll black over the ocean floor. Zones of self-knowledge like this, sinking and subtly transforming, seem to form the body of memory; how small daily actions are stirred by other, deeper motions that become clear only later. The glinting blue surface and the black rolling currents are the same body of water.

What is known and felt at the surface when you're eleven or twelve: One moment dissolves into the next as you breathe and move forward, printing the meanings of words upon smudged purple mimeographs in a fluorescent room, memorizing the periodic table and the chained pictures of chemical compounds, writing names inside the outlines of countries. You shake free of little hairs and lint the dark-green cotton sheet each morning, fold it back, smooth it with the side of a hand, plump the pillow, place it straight, then straighter. Or you sit dreamy on the toilet, peeing as you wind a strand of hair around your finger. Or smell your hair, dry and yellowish, dirty, baby shampoo, and wonder if that body down there beneath your chin will ever change, and rub two fingers along the skimpy skin over blue-bone ribs, close your hand slowly into a fist, admire the forearm's slight swelling muscle, then bend over to study the little bare cleft before dropping toilet paper into the bowl. You rake wet leaves in the backyard, smell stale coffee air when you come inside chilled and hurry to make your mother's bed before she's home from work, and slam the door at the bottom of the attic stairs, so that dust whorls float behind your dirty feet as you run up to the green cork room, the moss rug.

Beneath these streaming moments other things move silently, splashing up sometimes in dreams. *I was running down the hill again with that little man holding my hand. Who is he?* Surely no one at eleven thinks consciously of creating herself, of pulling in from all she sees and touches the most valuable strands. *To make my father see me, love me, this is what I have to do . . .* No. That he hadn't seen was too obliterating to articulate: that one father hadn't seen, and the other had left as well. But something in the body knows what it's doing, understands it's crucial to collect or discard strands among all you see, to build and weave and tighten. This is a critical venture because what you're making is *you*: devising ways to be valuable.

But if you're lucky, or just healthy enough, it's not only wanting to be valuable to a pair of fathers as remote as gods. It's working in a way that's unwittingly sane against being hollow or leaky, making your self *home* despite everything. Because there are options, and one is not to do this, not to carve a safe cell for yourself and fill it with things that are useful, but to give in and go under.

I stopped keeping a diary soon after New York and didn't write in another for three years. Maggy and I would speak to our father occasionally — on birthdays, for instance (*Although Daddy called I'm going to write a letter to him, anyway, to ask formally for some pamphlets on the U.N.*) — but we didn't go to New York again until Christmas, then Easter, then the following summer, and I think the girls visited their father as often. We saw the girls in New York and at Paul's; except maybe once, they did not stay with us, so we saw them only on their territory, and it felt as if there was a problem with our house or mother, a danger or an uncleanness from which the girls must be kept. New York felt all splendor and treat: chocolates on Madison Avenue, the U.N. building with its glass and bright flags, artist studios in cobblestone Soho, the Lincoln Center, dinners out. The girls would go to a private school while we'd go to a public junior high. They'd have a driver; we'd ride the bus. Their mother painted and arranged flowers on the Upper East Side, while ours was alone and took the bus to work. The girls seemed to have two fathers, we seemed to have none.

In August, when Maggy and I first returned from New York, our mother was still looking for a job. She'd sit in her bedroom in pink cutoffs and a bikini top, typing job applications to send out to the world. She was starting fresh, and who knew? Life might be waiting outside each morning when she

JANE ALISON

swung open the heavy front door. The oaks stood huge and green on Barnaby, the humid air veiling the street into September, and when she stepped outside she turned herself out, opened her bright sea eyes, looked to see what was out there. She was thirty-eight and had danced the cancan and might do it that instant if you dared her, right on the front walk in her flowered nightie as she paused to breathe the morning air, then picked up the paper to see what the day held.

Barnaby Woods was a lucky neighborhood to start over in, full of *Washington Post* writers, photographers, artists. My mother waved and helloed gaily over the hood of her new old beige Volkswagen, and soon she sat beautiful and wry amid the gatherings in the D'Angelos' garden up the street, drinking wine and talking about Archibald Cox or Rose Mary Woods's foot on the pedal, and we'd be there, too, we'd run barefoot up the sidewalk still warm from the day's heat, slide into that deep green garden, and lie on the grass, reaching for fireflies at dusk. When Nixon resigned the following summer, fireworks exploded on Barnaby Street. And the feel of those late summer nights, that smooth asphalt warm beneath my bare feet as I glided in the dusk and looked through the oak branches to the sky full of cool light, was like a wild current of life that tugged me outward and could pull me free from the nets of that family, make me something on my own, something else.

Paul came Fridays to take Tommy and Sundays to drop him off, but he existed otherwise at the end of the phone line, or the way Daddy had for so long: a black hole in my chest that was both numb and painful. When this second divorce was being worked out, or when Paul and my mother were still fighting whatever they hadn't finished, he'd call, and Maggy or I would hand the phone straight to our mother, who, stopping in the kitchen doorway amid bags of groceries, would clamp the receiver between ear and shoulder, motion with her chin for us to dump the frozen peas and carrots in boiling water, then pour gin over glass after glass of ice, her voice rising, body sinking, until finally she sat wedged in the doorway, weeping, cord kinking from her hand up the wall, while we sat silently putting forkfuls of vegetables and chicken pot pie into our mouths.

Paul had a legal commitment to Maggy and me in exchange, I gather, for my father's commitment to Patricia and Jenny. We still had Paul's nationality and name, sort of, although in the divorce documents of 1974 Maggy and I are called *Cummins* again. Also in these documents: She and I seem to be worth three-eighths as much as Tommy. In the house was a murky air of gratitude that anything came for us at all, given that we weren't Paul's daughters.

When he drove up to fetch or drop Tommy and deliver a check, he might also take down an air conditioner, examine a broken bike. My mother often was not there when he came, and Maggy would stay in her room with the door shut, so I'd be the one to let him in while Tommy looked for Red Dog. Paul would stand in the hall and glance around at the house he'd once lived in, at the old gold chair, the repaired dining-room set he'd bought with my mother, a painting he'd bought with her, too, then let her have or not wanted.

His eyes might move toward the kitchen, upstairs toward the bedroom where he'd once slept, perhaps think better of that journey, return. And while he was there, the wood floor he'd walked in on, and the stained cream carpet beneath his foot, and the musty brown striped sofa he sat on, and those wool curtains behind his dark head, and how clean they were or how worn or dusty, were not just themselves; they were my mother, Maggy, me, all left.

Sitting with my ankles crossed and cold hands under my legs, I'd feel myself defend that sofa or rug. It wasn't clear how to look at his eyes, it wasn't clear at all what to do.

"So how's your mother getting on, Jane?" he'd ask.

"Okay."

"Good, good. Your sister?"

"Fine."

"The car still acting up?"

"It's all right."

He'd nod, seeming satisfied, interview over. Then pull a check from his pocket, look at me so I'd take note as he placed it on the chest beneath an Indonesian figurine, and walk with his son out the door.

He sure is generous in the way of birthday presents! I got a stamper which makes my name, a set of stationery which has my name and address on it, 12 colored pencils which have my name . . .

A gravitational puzzle, repelling and pulling at once. Or like the black disk that glows in your eyelids when you've looked at the sun: still there and burning, but not there at all.

———

My mother got a job with the government, teaching grammar, writing, and communications for $12,000 a year, and we fell into order around her. We cooked macaroni, vacuumed and dusted the living room each weekend, cleaned the bathroom, swept the stairs, folded laundry, babysat neighborhood kids for $1 an hour; I ran a day-camp in the basement, tacking signs about it on all the Barnaby oaks. We bought our clothes at Penney's and Encore. The energy crisis began, so we kept the thermostat low, and when icicles formed inside my attic windows, we taped sheets of plastic over them, sealing me in. The huge oaks in the backyard dropped thousands of leaves onto the mud, where they rotted and formed sodden mats, and acorns pelted the roof, then sank into the swampy leaves and put out tough slippery roots so that rot layered the backyard in prehistoric growth that was heavy and pungent and slippery with slugs, and this must be raked up, could not take over, like the bills on the orange chest, like the dining room ceiling suddenly crashing in, the kind of thing that threatened the house with collapse, as if only a force of will could keep it standing. So after school I'd rake. For weeks I'd drop my books on the yellow kitchen table and go back and face it, the sea. I'd stuff leaves in black plastic bags with my boot, but the acorns and twigs poked through the plastic and ripped it, so that by the time I dragged one sodden bag from the end of the yard by the alley all the way up to the house, through the side zone wet with ivy and nervous with daddy longlegs, and up to the sidewalk, the hole would have caught on roots and rocks and ripped wider, and half the leaves would have fallen out and left a trail of failure, and sometimes this new world was just too exhausting.

Those years feel larval. Not just because of the wet leaves and maggots squirming beneath them and the little white worms that wiggled out of the bread-dough figures I'd hung on my cork walls, but because the split in South America and then the trip to New York had been shocking, had left me a weak underground thing. Now at school being white was a problem. My body did not grow but stayed a pale tube I hid in ugly magenta corduroy pants, old hiking boots, a thick Andean sweater. But larval times are times of waiting: storing up and waiting.

Maggy and I took the M4 each morning to Alice Deal Junior High. The school stood in a leafy white neighborhood of Georgian and Tudor houses and groomed gardens, the houses bigger and gardens more lavish than in Barnaby Woods. But only a handful of kids from that plush neighborhood went to Deal, which was big and brick and smelled of urine on hot heaters, sweet hair pomades, warm gas from the stoves in Home Economics, cigarettes, pot, and incense to hide it. The black kings and queens who ruled Deal came from parts of D.C. like Anacostia and Northeast, far from that leafy place, arriving on school or city buses.

On the first day, they felt like a monsoon, a warm, dark storm coming in the front and back doors of the M4, with purple picks in their hair, snapping gum, smoking, eyeing us hard, wearing platform shoes that could tromp you. They kept coming up the steps and pushing down the aisle, and I could not understand it, wondered if all these people could be from the same family, because the brain has compartments and mine were stupidly small. The M4 doors wheezed shut, and we sagged up Nebraska to Deal, the nine white kids with their big baby teeth staring at their scared fish reflections in the windows, trying to melt into the glass.

I was the only white girl in Home Ec., one of four or five in Gym. Between classes in the crowded halls it was good to be small like me because newspapers would be rolled up with sand, slung tight, and used to whack blond heads that showed. Packed halls, though, were better than empty ones, much better than when some teacher sent you on an errand to the other end of school and the halls were empty, but not really empty, not in the stairwells, behind doors. *Hey white girl. White girl! What you got in that bag. Give me that.* Those words *white girl* were sometimes said so slowly, each morsel held long in the mouth and hated, but sometimes spat out fast as a smack. In Gym, I flattened myself against the lockers when I pulled off my shirt and slipped on the horrible soft blue-nylon gym suit, while around me dark breasts and pregnant bellies sprang from brassieres and old panties: bodies fully made and shockingly potent already. *I tell you ladies: you got half as much hair in those pits as you got on your heads you had better shave that mess!* I had nothing in my pits, nothing anywhere, twenty-four, twenty-four, twenty-four, and was knocked down easily with a medicine ball by a beautiful girl named Corinthia, and was even knocked down with a *Webster's* thrown from a window: Something flapped at my head like a prehistoric bird and I fell to the sidewalk.

No cafeteria for the white kids at Deal. We huddled on

the blacktop in the cold, near the numbing iron rail, with our clammy sandwiches. We skidded down the steps and tramped over the muddy field, ever farther from the brick building, until we reached the edge of school grounds, the bushes and garbage and rats, and sat shivering there or around a sewer top. But it felt safer, because just the other side of a fence lay the curb and smooth street and trimmed hedges and paving stones of that fine neighborhood, like waking after a nightmare.

After school, the white kids who took the M4 bolted to the bus stop once the bell had rung, and we hoped to god it would come before the school buses finished loading and began to swing around the corner. Because when they did, lit cigarettes or rocks or bottles were pelted from the windows at us huddling like pale stupid sheep. A cigarette stuck burning in my arm once as I stood clutching my daisy-covered notebook, and I couldn't understand what it was, thought it was a bee. A friend was hit by a rock in the head, and she didn't get it, either, just stared at her bloody fingers through her glasses, confused. A skinny white boy had an arm and leg broken, another was given a concussion, a gym teacher was beaten up by girls. I never went to the bathroom at Deal, or at least not after the first times. I made myself not need to pee, and since my body stayed a narrow tube there was no other reason to go. *Hey girl. You a girl? What you got between those legs? Why you got no titties?*

When *Roots* aired, the hallways were plastered with posters showing fat white men whipping slaves, and for weeks tall afroed boys between thirteen and twenty strode the halls in tight purple pants and shiny gold shirts, shaking their fists and shouting "Kunta Kinte!" We knew we were guilty. We were guilty, weak, pale, and privileged, and they were righteous, stylish, strong. It was their school; we gave it up gladly. We sat in pale clumps at assemblies, as bits of ceiling plaster crumbled onto our heads, and watched them—beautiful cheerleaders with gleaming strong legs, spotlit afroed singers in sequins, spectacled class officers; we watched. One day the doors at both ends of the main hall were propped open as a line of girls with glittering platform shoes and fist-shaped pink picks in the pockets of their hot pants did the Bump from one end of school to the other, a sinuous line of girls slowly rolling their hips and shoulders and kicking out their fabulous shoes, smiling low-lidded with their fabulous names, Corinthia, Shantelle, VeLores, and this is the most beautiful thing I ever saw there. *Green is the land! Red is the blood! Black are the people!*

I threaded my way like a silverfish, hunting *A*'s and stars, learning how to bake cornbread and do the Bump in secret, slowly growing a more opaque skin as I held my eyes straight, never needed to pee, stopped flinching when I heard *white girl*.

Larval, underground, waiting: That's how those first years in Washington seem. But they were also lit by making things. Turning inward, compiling. I spooned flour into a measuring cup to bake brownies, cut with long, slicing scissors orange cloth for a pattern, smelled my mother's warm Singer as the wheel spun, the pedal humming underfoot. Stitching a hem by hand, or typing: useful things to do, and soothing, because you know that each minute you spend in these measured motions is good, productive, nothing wrong. Making things helps make you. And there were the things I made in my attic room with its green cork walls and mossy rug, a rug I'd saved $35 babysitting to buy from a classified. The most intimate relations, just me and the lamp and a pile of paper or pastels or glass slides, my face close and breathing by the hot bulb, absorbed. I did Gothic calligraphy when a boyfriend of my mother's gave me a book and fountain pen; I wrote and illustrated greeting cards that my mother took to show and sell to everyone at work. I invented things—the word *invention* made me thrill: project! An orange peeler constructed from a pair of wooden salad servers affixed with razors, a candy dispenser like a pinball game; neither worked. But I won a science-fair ribbon for a plasticine mouth—red lips, pink tongue thrust between gapped teeth—that illustrated zones of taste buds. Sweet, sour, bitter, salty. I was obsessed with valences, nomenclature, charts. Opposites *must* neutralize each other, so for weeks after school in the kitchen I mixed portions of sugar and lemon juice, trying to find the balance that turned the two to water. I covered index cards with the periodic table and names of the phyla of Animalia to memorize even when brushing my teeth.

I drew a chart of our family, too. It made the situation easier to explain when anyone asked if I had sisters or brothers, and I kept this card in my wallet. *See, my father and mother and this other couple switched. I've got a double in New York. See?* The chart had lines and arrows. Girls with hair as straggly as mine looked at the chart and then at me as we stood on the windy field at Deal, eating liverwurst sandwiches, and I don't know what they saw. Someone gave me an acrylic cube for displaying photos, and what else to display but the family? But with only six sides the cube posed a paradox: Who could be included, who not? Paul was the first to cut; that was clear. Paul, and of course with him, myself. That left eight. Did I have to display pictures of the family I lived with? How could I have Helen on my desk and not my mother? The betrayal made me queasy. And on top of this numerical puzzle was another: Which way to set the cube? Who would be smiling up, who face down? Finally I decided that if Paul was cut, Daddy should be, too, to be fair, to be even. I settled on having only girls and halfling boys — and Helen: as a pious act or amulet against danger, I don't know.

When the girls came to Washington to see Paul, he often invited us down for an evening — to make it more of a party, be a nice guy, watch us in action, who knows. Maggy and I would take the bus down Connecticut, or Paul would come and drive us through Rock Creek Park, or Maggy would decide she wouldn't go, why should she. Often I'd go alone. Tommy would already be there, little amphibian, caught between the half sisters who belonged to his father and the half sisters who belonged to his mother, caught between his father's new marriage and us.

Paul lived for a time in one apartment and then moved to another near Dupont Circle, and that's the one I remember. In a neat, modern building, it was clean and cool, with a wall of windows, white carpeting, a big potted ficus, glass and steel and leather furniture, high-quality sound. His new wife was like him: tennis, work, scotch, the news; the apartment was cold and orderly. The girls would stay in the study, that apartment not made for such creatures with their bright plumage and mess, but they'd have been there, with Tommy, unwrapping presents because it was always a holiday and watching gory films and eating chips and getting more inflamed and loud. Then I would appear, with stringy hair and old brown bell-bottoms, there only thanks to my relation to Tommy and to Paul's sense of duty, there by charity. I was scrawny and sulky and defensive, an orphan. Tommy never seemed sure how to greet me.

"So how's school going, Jane," Paul might say after I'd handed over the wrapped tie or whatever sorry Christmas or birthday present I'd bought him at Woodies, he'd opened it and thanked me solemnly, and I'd slid down in the black leather chair and been given a Coke. Even a question about school led nowhere good. I was an easy mark, and so often when I was there the girls seemed to want to put on a show for the emperor, to talk about "the blacks" at Deal and "the blacks" who overran Washington, the way he did. I'd be spooked by those cries of *Kunta Kinte!* and walk right into their trap.

"You're not supposed to call them that."

"What's wrong with *the blacks*?" one of the girls might say. "What then, *coloreds? Negroes?* Why don't you just call them what they are, Jane? Niggers!"

I'd flush, cross my arms, stare at my Coke.

"Oh, come on, Jane. Do it. Just say the word!"

I'd cross my arms tighter and look hard out the window.

"Jane's afraid if she says *nigger* some enormous black man will come looming up."

"Like a shark! She's terribly afraid of sharks, you know, Father."

He'd raise his eyebrows and sit back, grinning.

"She's petrified that if she says *nigger* some enormous black man carrying a club will come looming up and beat her!"

Of course I was, who wouldn't be? People got beat up all the time! So I'd shake my head hard and press my lips tight, and Paul and his daughters and son — sweet traitor — would laugh, their cheeks blotchy and thrilled, and Jenny suddenly hoisted herself up from the sofa and made a face that was half shark, half big black man, staring dead ahead and doing something awful with her lips, and came hulking over the thick white carpet to me, and I stared hard through the wall, until she threw herself on the carpet and shrieked.

After a while, to quiet things down: a change of subject.

"So, Jane," Paul might say. "How's your mother getting on?"

Fast answer. "Fine."

"Good, good." A sip, a pause, a glance around the room, as if summoning the audience, the lynchers. "How's her job? What's she doing now—" and he'd squint and strain, as if trying to extract the information out of the muck of her life "—what is it she's doing again? Teaching government *blacks* how not to talk *black*? Teaching them how to *write*?"

And up would go his brows in disbelief, and out would

belt howls of laughter from the girls, and heat would rise through my brown bell-bottoms, and I'd slide down furious in the Mies van der Rohe chair.

The only good class I had at Deal that year was science with Mrs. Rountree, where we did chemical equations, *hydrogen helium lithium beryllium boron carbon nitrogen oxygen,* memorizing positive and negative valences, seeing what chemical would neutralize another, what chemical made another explode.

Another pause and jingle of ice, another shift of subject.

"Your mother still seeing — what's his name — Phil? Bill?"

She probably was, Phil or Bill or Bob or Ken or some John or another. Men pulled up in white Cadillacs on Friday or Saturday and took her to dinner at Picadilly, she would dance out all Givenchy, leggy blue dress, bright gap-toothed smile, and what was so hard to work out, as I sat on Paul's slick black chair and dug my feet into that hateful white carpet and looked at all those bright brown eyes and laughing straight American teeth, was the right way to answer, how to know whether my mother would have a positive valence for attracting these men or a negative valence for needing to. Everyone seemed interested. Paul, because he'd been married to her, and the girls because they were thirteen and fourteen and the subject was not only sex but sex involving that famous woman who might or might not have taken their father but in any case had failed to keep him. And given how much intimate knowledge of my mother and Paul existed in the girls' principal household, who knows how much speculation there had been as to why my mother and Paul's marriage had failed, who knows how many stories had been told altogether. After a visit to Washington, the girls surely reported to Daddy and Helen. No one wrote letters anymore. The diplomatic pouch was moot; now we had the Northeast Corridor. Now we ourselves were diplomats, spies, shuttling between New York and D.C. My mother wanted to know about my father and Helen and about Paul and his new wife, their apartments and clothes and what they made for dinner. And although my father and Helen asked few questions about her, they seemed to listen closely to our answers and watch us for clues; we were documents of her, after all, and of the failed marriage between her and Paul, just as Patricia and Jenny must prove their own success: The girls *had* to, like racehorses on which everything was staked. And Paul might ask how my mother was getting on, but he seemed really to want to know about Helen and Edward, especially the intelligence I might offer but his own girls wouldn't, because our allegiances were different.

I sat there in the black leather chair and tried to figure out the only right answer, the best portrait of my mother for the different agendas, and Tommy looked pulled to pieces as he sat in his chair clutching his fifth Coke, shaking the ice in it, grinning, inflamed, looking from one of us to the other, his knee jerking hectically, helpless.

But when I left, the entertainment surely changed, and another cat was thrown into the pen. Evidence burned later in the girls' eyes.

The fact of the matter *is,* I picture Paul saying to his girls, slow and authoritative when it was time to get to the point; the fact of the matter *is* that Jane goes to a much tougher school than you two. She doesn't get driven down to a *private* school by a chauffeur and spend all day with a bunch of prissy rich kids. What she's doing is much, much harder. And just look at how well *she's* doing. First prize in that poster contest, and that science fair, too. A smart kid, he might say, and pause, and regard them. Then shake his head in admiration. Just terrifically smart.

And I can see him lean back and give his girls that challenging look, his girls so steeped in Edward and Helen. And I can see his eyes fixed hard on theirs as he says these things and slowly swims backward, ever deeper, farther out of their reach, and would they rise to the challenge, earn the right not to drown?

Maybe Jenny had traveled to Washington arrayed like a bride with all her fresh honors, hoping, without saying so, to be *seen,* restored. Maybe she'd gazed out the Amtrak window as the Philadelphia boathouses floated by, and listed the private items she'd stored: the medals for riding, the papers, the prizes. Maybe she even thought up things to say, or practiced jokes, moving phrases around in her mouth. And then maybe, a week later, she found that she still couldn't win what she needed, it kept gliding away, and she traveled back to New York growing fiercely reckless, her breath hot and fast on the glass.

And often I was in New York when she returned, in her pink room, waiting. Each time I'd have arrived with my own pile to heap at my father's feet: straight *A*'s again, my name on the honor roll, that science-fair ribbon, that poster-contest prize. I would throw down my clanking medals, stand in the dust, and wait. I don't know what I thought winning my father would look like — would he suddenly see me, take my hand, say, You are my own girl?

In their silken bedroom with its big, bright paintings and view of the park, would my father and Helen have discussed the situation, once several months had gone by and enough information had been gathered to suggest how to proceed? Did they say, Well, does Paul single out and prefer his own girls? Hardly: Just look at the state they were in whenever they came home, the state they were getting in altogether. Then my father could not single out his girls, either: the only appropriate policy.

So as I stood there waiting, my medals heaped at his feet, it was as if each little medal of mine undid one of Jenny's or did damage to the house, and he would nod, look embarrassed, and a glance would dart between him and Helen: I was boasting, which was to be discouraged. To single out a girl was not fair. And it was a little sad, wasn't it, how *obsessed* Jane was with achievement and *knowing* things and *competing,* and why on earth did she think it mattered?

Again Jenny and I lay side by side in twin beds, breathing hotly the nighttime air. We whispered about analogous evolution, insects, molluscs, the lineages in mythology, elements, every name and system we knew. Maybe we loved these Linnean worlds. But I think mostly we whispered what we knew because each item I knew but she didn't could erase her, and each item she knew, me.

It would have been better if we hadn't both wanted what we did, or if we hadn't been so much the same, if one of us had been stupid or sweet; if we hadn't both apparently grown up craving, in secret, the attention of a man very far away and evolving the exact same means to get him; if our tissues hadn't been made of pure jealousy. Because it didn't take long for us to know that neither might ever win her own father, that we both might starve, and that made our struggles all the more bitter.

In my science class at Deal we looked through microscopes at euglenas and paramecia — their nuclei, cilia, fine long flagella — and we learned about seeds, corn kernels, genetics. I had a microscope at home, a small one in a wooden box with a brass clasp that one of my mother's boyfriends had given me — anyone who lasted until our birthdays or Christmas brought us gifts — and I'd study a drop of stream water, or strand of hair, or fly's wing. Our dicotyledonous family should be just as explicable. I'd sit in my attic room, at my desk made of such soft balsalike wood that a ballpoint pen pushed hard in the right place could pop through the grain, and I'd trace out the family traits. As with kernels of corn, there were genetic systems that made my stepsisters mean, me so maddeningly weak. I drew charts.

Edward and Rosemary had produced Margaret and Jane; Paul and Helen had produced Patricia and Jenny. All four girls were pretty enough, and this made sense because so were all the parents. All four girls were smart, and this made sense, too. But our side of the family, I felt, was *nicer*. For Mrs. Rountree's class I had to collect a hundred different leaves, pin them to pages, and classify them, so every warm Sunday my mother drove me to the National Arboretum, spread out a blanket on the grass in the sun, and read the paper, looking up at me, smiling and shielding her eyes, as I trooped by plucking leaves. Mostly she was good and *nice*—in a drought, she would look at shriveled shrubs and wince; after dinner she'd take us for walks to the Beautiful Alley, just to love the azaleas and the evening sky; in a field once, at a picnic, she suddenly cried out to a cow, "Hello! Hello! Moo!" and we imitated her for days, for years. And my father seemed only proper and distant, hopeful eyes blinking as he jingled his change—but then again, how would I know. It didn't seem that the Australian side was downright *mean* the way the girls could be, so this trait surely belonged to the Americans. Another American trait was strong, even, white teeth, which both Paul and Helen had, not crooked and dun teeth like my parents', so it made irritating sense that the girls' teeth were better. The test case would be the little boys, the hybrids, each partaking of a different combination of the same parents. Through them you'd be able to see whether meanness or strong teeth were sex-linked traits. If Tommy got good teeth but Nicholas didn't, then that had been one of Paul's traits, not Helen's, or the condition of strong teeth was itself not stronger than the condition of weak teeth; the parent with weak teeth could counteract the parent with strong teeth, and the child they produced would have cavities, and this *was* the case with Tommy, so maybe . . .

One thing I worried about especially was whether the

American parents had stronger genes altogether, whether they were just plain stronger, because this would mean the girls would be, too. And then there was the problem of what *strong* meant, whether power was something you could *make* in yourself or simply *had,* whether you really had it anyway or if it was draped upon you from outside and could be stripped away again. And in love, which was most powerful: attracting or keeping? Or refusing to need?

What exactly made the woman in one envelope of skin so valuable, so golden, that she could pull a man from his family, she could become all he saw? And what made another worth nothing?

For two years, in her pink bedroom, Jenny and I fought on. I don't think we could have told you why; it just drove us like blood in veins. We performed ever more elaborate neurotic routines. We took pictures of each other in the dark with flash bulbs; one of us would shoot blind while the other posed in the flare. When I developed mine, I found that in the first pictures Jenny had done the same gags as me — lain back with her head and arms flung over the mattress, dead, or stood on her head, or crossed her eyes — but the last pictures are different. In one she stands before me with her face cold and gives me the finger; in another she rears above me with scissors.

In the dark we whispered at each other, fierce. She lay spread-eagled on her pink bed and listed names of gastropods while I lay spread-eagled on my pink bed and listed names of arthropods. Kingdom phylum class order family genus species! Hymenoptera Lepidoptera Coleoptera Orthoptera! The *-ptera* part means wing! So *lepidoptera* means scale wing because *lepido* means scale! And *hymenoptera* means membrane wing because the wing's like a membrane!

I had to outdo her. But she was older and went to a real school and it was impossible that I could know more. One day — as if a switch flipped, and she with her extra year could decide this, or maybe she simply gave up the battle — she flounced over in bed and announced that it was boring and childish to keep raving like this, she simply couldn't *give* a piss! And she gazed into the more mature, dusky air around her and shrugged a bored shoulder and said that the fact of the matter *was,* none of the sort of thing I was chattering about mattered. But speaking of Hymenoptera, probably I didn't even know what a *hymen* was. Did I? And what about *orgasm?* Did I happen to know what an orgasm was?

It sounded like *organism,* I didn't know, and I flailed around trying to answer until she snorted with satisfaction, fell back on her bed, and stretched her arms toward the ceiling, languorous, while on my bed I lay in flames.

The next day she informed me, kindly, that the fact of the matter *was* that I was oversensitive, everyone could see it, they'd discussed it in fact quite recently, she and Patricia and Daddy and Mum, and she knew Father thought so, too.

They'd discussed it in fact quite recently: a glimpse through the mirror at how the others saw us or wanted to see us. A corollary of the formal photos they'd sent, a curious reflection of ourselves. Glimpses of their stories over the years: *Jane is utterly emotionless and cold . . . Mum's the first to have been able to please Daddy . . . Jane will never be as close to Daddy as we are, and never as close to Father, either.*

Paul still came up Fridays to get Tommy, Sundays to drop him off, and while Tommy looked in the closet for his rocks or comics, I was still the one to greet Paul. He'd rap on the screen door and stand shadowed behind it, and I'd let him in, go fetch him a beer. He'd sit, rest an ankle on a knee, stretch an arm along the back of the brown sofa, look around at the house he'd once lived in.

I'd hand him the beer. I'd sit down and wait.

"So, how is everything, Jane."

"Okay."

He'd nod, take a sip, ask the other usual questions.

"School as terrific as always?" At which I'd roll my eyes and say something smart, and he'd laugh and hold me lit in his sight.

Then he might lean back and slide into the real topic of interest. "So, Jane: There's nothing you don't pick up, you're so goddamned *observant*. Tell me. What do you *really* think about all of them —" a gesture northward with his chin "— all of them up there on Fifth Avenue?" And he'd lift his brows, give a conspiratorial smile, welcome whatever intelligence I'd spill. And of course I'd spill, reckless and hungry, I'd spill anything to hold that attention.

When Jenny and I reached fourteen and thirteen, the terms of battle shifted. She herself changed, everything sprouted, breasts, blood, hair, all that potent female stuff, while my body stayed underground, my head floating full of nomenclatures above it. We were like different kinds of fish, one throwing out flamboyant color and preposterous membranes, the other forming a spiny skin like rock.

She was now tall and curvy in a yellow bikini, and even her face had become more sly, her mouth a sweet, pink della Francesca curl like her mother's. She looked around everywhere with bright, hot eyes; she turned upon herself and learned arts of her body. In New York she led me into her bathroom and shut the door. "You've got to shave your legs," she said.

"Why?"

She shrugged. "Because that's bloody revolting. Here," she said. "Put your foot here."

I put my foot on the sink, and Jenny soaped her hand, lathered my calf, pulled the razor in a clean stroke over the skin, and knocked it against the sink, the soft blond hairs running into clots.

"Watch it," I said as she slid the razor fast along my stony ankle, stinging. She laughed and made a sweet face in the mirror: as if she'd meant to *hurt* me, her darling sister.

Jenny stood at the mirror with her hips thrust forward and applied lipstick, shadow, powder. She put them on me, too, holding my jaw between her fingers. "God, no one's shown you how to do *anything*," she said, pinching my mouth open like a snapdragon and stroking on red.

No, no one had. My mother's beauty was natural, and otherwise, who could bother? She'd walk around her room naked as I lay listless on her double bed, the one she'd slept on with Paul, and he'd slept on with Helen, and I'd take to college and sleep on with I don't know how many men until I finally left it somewhere and moved. I'd lie on her bed and study her belly, her bottom. She'd give her hair a quick brush, slather the same lotion on her face as her legs. Helen I saw only fully composed. Nature versus art supreme: the emu and the peacock.

In her bathroom Jenny poofed me with powder and turned me to the mirror. "There." She took a handful of my hair, bunched it up, let it fall. She put more lipstick on her own mouth and pursed into the mirror. Then she grabbed me by the waist and held me, smiled, and kissed me hard on the cheek, her teeth pressing through lips and skin to bone.

"Now you're finished," she said, smiling at the lipstick bruise on my cheek.

She blossomed on the sidewalk, tossing her hair and exchanging looks with boys who only emerged from trees or shop windows when I saw them staring at Jenny. Once she'd caught their eye, she lifted her chin and dropped them cold. They sneered or cursed but turned for another look, and that's when she smiled most. One boy riding by on a bike grabbed her breast, right on Fifth Avenue. She looked enraged, delighted, her face lit with excitement as she shook her fist and shouted, "My *god*! *Piss* on you, you bloody fucking P.R.!"

She was her own object now, her own show. At Gimbels she fingered scarves and sprayed perfumes and tried on hats, and then at Papaya King, sipping Coconut Champagne, she

opened her jacket, pulled out a gold-cased lipstick, and set
it on the counter. Then a pair of costume earrings, the price
tag still dangling. She placed them between the mustard and
napkins as people walked up or down Lexington the other
side of the grimy glass. She turned to me, grinning.

"You're an idiot."

She shrugged and twisted open the lipstick. "What shit!"
And dropped it magenta-head first into the trash can.

"So why did you take it?"

"Why shouldn't I?"

"You didn't even want it."

She laughed. "That's hardly the point." And looked away,
grew dreamy, abstracted, lowering her lids privately, but even
then surely feeling my eyes cold on her cheek. And which
was the greater potency, to feel eyes clinging to your skin, or
make marks on someone else's?

Beside me on a city sidewalk, Jenny was always ahead
now, gazing off into a more exotic air moving with subtle
currents. On a glaring road at the beach, her body oiled in
the yellow bikini, she turned herself out, her eyes aware of
her lean flesh shining as she strutted in her blue Dr. Scholl's.
She held her chin high, narrowed her eyes like Corinthia at
Deal, and sauntered, kicking out each bare gleaming leg in
a way that drove me wild and was exactly how Paul walked,
and Patricia, and Tommy, because those American genes
were so strong. Suddenly I couldn't stand it and imitated,
throwing up my chin and flinging each leg out, letting the
heel of my red Dr. Scholl's clop like a camel to annoy her.
She smiled; she ignored me. She looked like she knew her

skin was magnetic and all eyes would fly to her, and sometimes they did. But if they didn't she'd make them. One day on that road at the beach she grabbed a little boy by the neck and kissed him hard, as she'd kissed me, and left him on the hot asphalt, crying.

My mother had joined groups with names like Parents Without Partners, and she went to therapy and worried about possible *ramifications* from the situation with the fathers, as she called it. She wanted me to open up and tell her what I felt. I told her I did not feel a thing.

"Oh, of *course* you do! *Janie.*"

Nope, not a thing.

"You have to let yourself *feel!*" she would cry. "You can't bottle everything up!"

We would be playing Scrabble some hot summer night, and I'd be sitting on the old sofa, itching, and as I assembled some six-letter word, she would probe at me.

"Darling. Jane. *Listen* to me."

I'd turn to stone.

She'd finally make me put down my wooden letters or stop adding the score, and she'd take my cold wrists and gaze at me with her big gray eyes and beg me to say what I *felt* about things, about, oh, *all* of it, the whole situation! She'd swing her head around like a horse in the rain, and exactly that subject, the whole situation, the situation with the fathers, the weakness implicit in it and feeling anything about it, was what I did not want to let show or have anything to do with. And as she gazed at me, kneading my thin wrists

with her thumbs, her own eyes filled with tears and there was
nothing I could do to stop this, her eyes filled and filled until
they spilled over, and I shut my eyes hard and put my arms
around her damp shoulders as she wept and shook and said,
"You know, none of this has been very easy for *me*, either."

Feeling, hunger, need: all weak. The object was to be hard,
to be marble. Not to blush like a white girl, not to cry, not
to be a girl at all. Because for one thing weakness was repulsive. And what was repulsive naturally repelled people, and if
you repelled people they wouldn't want you, and this unfor-
tunately took you back to the beginning, to admitting there
was something you needed. Unless you could transform your
object: Get everyone to want you but then not need them
at all.

What I truly loved, so easily, because there were no allegiances to be broken, was summertime dusk and the feeling
that came with it. The transparent feel of gliding over warm
asphalt with bare feet, with Tommy, walking down twilit
Barnaby to the Beautiful Alley, which cut a swath of coral
azalea through the block. I loved looking in windows as we
walked past, slipping through the glass and into lit rooms
and even for a moment into a little girl, watching a lean gray
cat stretch and roll on the sidewalk, losing my self, coming
home exhausted and fresh, stepping back into my body.

I loved dusk and its inner equivalent, that suspended
feeling when I wrote or drew. My father had given me a ream
of stationery with the little emu and kangaroo at the top,
and I covered sheet after sheet with green or blue marker.

I'd invent stories about slipping through mirrors to somewhere else, places like Narnia, reached by pushing through fur coats that became fir trees, or by gazing at the shadow of a boat gliding alongside you, willing yourself through water. I'd draw or paint, the distance between me and what I drew dissolving as my eyes traveled over each curve and my hand tried to remake it.

And then there was the painful, pulling beauty of the world itself: the rolling marbled sky, the glassy green underside of a wave. This beauty exists nowhere but the current of air between the object and your eyes, and you dissolve in that current, you become the seeing itself so long as you stand there and give yourself up. Beauty enters through the eyes and undoes you; it sets you loose from your self, lets you flow out and be other, and this I wanted most.

On weekends I took the bus downtown to a Washington torn up, the streets planked over while the subway was tunneled. It was like bouncing on the boardwalk, feet making that same warm, hollow sound, but here was no sand or sea, just Pennsylvania Avenue or F Street, abandoned. I went to the Smithsonian and looked at rocks, dinosaur bones, ancient clocks; I went to the National Gallery and ran up the cool marble steps to the greenery and fountain and poised, pointing Mercury; I took painting classes at the Corcoran. Years later, in my twenties, I studied there again, took a class in animation, and made a short film of Daedalus taking flight. A simple method, just drawing sheet upon sheet clipped to a register, each showing a sixteenth of a second of motion, a tiny move in knee and wing. Making these drawings on the

Murphy table in my studio in Adams Morgan, a table with benches that unfolded like a wooden insect from the wall, I wouldn't notice time itself passing, real time measured by the sun. I wouldn't move or look up as I sat and drew each sixteenth of a second, just got lost in the motions I drew, so that three or four hours would pass and the sunlight would have slid over the parquet floor, out the window and down to the sidewalk, to the hoods of the Ethiopians' cabs, and while that had happened I'd gotten Daedalus to take one step. But I'd thought about him and envisioned Icarus in the air: the feel of his arms straining, his knees loose in the wind, the sun blinding his eyes and melting the wax in hot drops on his shoulders, and the shocking sight of his shadow on the water rushing up as he falls in.

Always it felt polar, antipodal. When we were far enough away from those others the gravitational tug weakened, and I might almost be free, my own self. But seeing them was to be pulled under, Jenny and me forever in twin beds, wanting to cut ourselves out of that room, shake off that stifling other.

The summers my father lived in New York he rented beach houses on Shelter Island and Cape Cod, and Paul rented beach houses, too. All four girls went, with one brother or the other. There are pictures: Four swimsuited girls do handstands on a lawn, three shapely young females and me. Four girls array themselves on a boulder around Daddy, and he looks too young to possess these brimming creatures; it's alarming to look at this picture. Four girls on a dock perch on four wood posts, Daddy in the middle, our gymnastic legs stretching to reach him. *Watch me, Daddy! Daddy, look!* Each of us strains to be noticed, and except for me we are big girls now, women. We made up dances, put our arms around each other's shoulders and kicked and hopped like cancan girls. *Ask any mermaid you happen to see —*

The dock was gray, the shingled house was gray, the sky was gray, too — although in a print Helen made of us girls on the dock, the sky around us blazes orange. I remember my father preparing bait on the sand, lifting a worm and dangling it before us so we'd shriek.

I've dissected worms, I wanted to say. Don't you know? You stick one pin in the head and one at the end and take a scalpel and cut down the long squelching middle. Then you peel the gray-pink membrane away and pin that like wings to the board, leaving quivering strands: the alimentary tract, the nervous system. And I've collected insects, I wanted to say, and pinned them and labeled them; I know the classifications. And I know Spanish. And I can draw. I get all the prizes! Why don't you know this? Why don't you want to?

Instead I said, "Can I fish, too?"

Jenny stepped forward and plucked a worm from the bucket. "Me, too," she said. "Here! Here, Daddy."

But he shook his head and stepped away. Three was too many. He'd just fish alone.

So we danced. *Let Noxzema cream your face — da da da da —* We sang and kicked, each of us trying to kick highest, Rockettes. A bevy of beauties, an old man remarked when we went out together, my father and Helen walking ahead with Nicholas, the king and queen and sweet little prince, while the four girls jostled and squawked behind. *What a bloody racket comes from you lot!*

"People probably look at us and think, My god, they sure must have wanted a boy," Helen said once, and we laughed. But looking back now at us squawking and worthless, I think it was true. A boy, a boy. If the children who'd been left at that split had been boys, how different. A boy might still be owned by a father, even at a distance. A father might still really want him.

With all that hopping and kicking we were careful, on the dry splintering dock, to wear sandals. But on the sand we kicked barefoot and free.

"Watch us! Watch us, Daddy!"

We thumped on the sand, all four in sync, kicking.

Let Noxzema cream your face — da da da da —

Suddenly there was a scream and a crumple, and if it didn't happen right then, as I recall, it did happen that summer and was a sign of change that's documented in the last of these photos: the bandaged foot.

A scream, and Jenny had gone down; she'd landed on a broken bottle or shell, and a piece of her foot flapped, blood spilling.

"Mum!" Patricia screamed up the beach. "Daddy!"

Jenny held her leg bent close to peer into the gash while we stood around her, clutching our hands. "Look at all the blood!" she said. "Can you believe it?" And she stared at that fascinating thing, her insides, the potency of her split skin.

Daddy put her in the car and drove her away, and she gazed back at us, triumphant, back at me standing there, a mute, raging statue.

I can keep everything inside of me until I explode.

She'd fainted, too, I realized later; she'd collapsed on the floor of the Natural History Museum, her blood slippery on the marble, and everyone crowded around to look. She had chanced upon something new. For a time we'd looked at each other in the mirror, too similar, no way to win. But now something darkened on her side of the glass, and on one side stood a princess, on the other a grinning witch.

Corresponding scenes a few hundred miles down the coast, in Delaware, this time at the beach house Paul rented. It was my beach, where I'd nearly drowned, but it was Paul's house and car and money and plan, and he was the girls' father, so the beach was theirs now. Again four oiled girls in bikinis gathered around a man, a tall, tanned man with an arrogant walk; we came squawking after him down the boardwalk like geese.

It was terribly kind of Father, the girls told me, to invite Maggy and me as well. Because he wasn't obliged to, after all. Now that he wasn't even our stepfather.

And it was really rather generous of *them,* they added, not to mind if we came along.

We spread out the matching towels Daddy and Helen had given us — the gifts they gave us always matched — the towels printed with huge butterflies, each a different color, pink, yellow, blue, except, this time, for mine; there hadn't been

four butterfly towels, I guess, so they gave me one with leop-
ard spots and red and green racing stripes, a distinction that
made me wildly proud. We spread out our towels on the soft,
burning sand and placed ourselves on them, in bikinis, skin
gleaming. We lay flat, toes east, the sounds of waves crashing
and songs in the air, Coppertone and coconut, blazing sky.
I'm not in love . . .
We lay melting in the heat, singing silently, dreaming.
Ooh, you'd wait a long time for me . . . And when a low, praising
whistle came from the boardwalk, we tilted our heads back,
bared our necks, to see: Paul stood up there, laughing, his
face dark against the sky, and which of us was he looking at
the most?

Late one day, Jenny and I walked along the beach as a storm
approached, after the lifeguards had whistled and shut the
beach because of lightning. We went out anyway, as the sky
darkened and the wind rose. We were fourteen and thirteen
and excited as we stood on the sand in the whipping wind
and looked into the wild sky, the rough sea. We climbed out
one of the long rock jetties, slippery with seaweed and sharp
with barnacles, as the waves sprayed our faces, and I'm sure
Jenny went farther because she always went farther, gripping
a rock with her toes, lurching forward and catching herself
on another sharp rock with her hands, skinning her shin and
cursing and shaking her leg until the sting went, looking
through her blowing hair at the ocean. For a time we stood
there, unsteady, each on a wet rock, and felt full of that wild
sea wind, ecstatic.

"The sea!" she cried. "The power of the sea!" She turned back to me, the sky flashing and dark behind her. "Doesn't it just —" and she couldn't even finish, just threw out her arms and stared at the thrashing water and looked like she wanted to fly into it, be undone, set loose by it, like me.

That was August 1975. She and my father and the rest of his family had lived on the same continent as we did for two years. But a few months later my father was posted back home. When he told us they were leaving, I didn't know what to say. I hadn't realized that could happen; I'd thought there would be more time.

When Maggy and I left New York the last time, I think my father came down the escalator at Penn Station to put us on the train, as usual, then went out to the platform. He probably walked along peering through the tinted windows to find us and, when he did, smiled and stood with his hands in his pockets, rocking back and forth on his feet. Maybe he wrote one of his messages on the glass with his finger, or made a sad face and wiped his eyes, and maybe, as usual, when the conductors whistled and the doors slid shut, he mimed alarm, and when the train began moving he jogged alongside us, lifting his knees and elbows comically high. He probably did all of this again, and again it seemed that he was nearer than he'd been during the visit, nearer than he'd been in our lives.

We had taken pictures that last time. It was New Year's Eve. These pictures are new versions of those from ten years earlier, by Lake Burley Griffin, where my father kneels between Maggy and me like a groom. Now the three of us sit side by side near a window overlooking the park, in wintry afternoon light. Maggy and I are old enough to look like him, the light giving our three faces the same curving nose, serious mouth, troubled eyes. We look alike as we sit side by side here, but not as though we know each other well or are comfortable close together. Maggy has placed an old Canberra picture next to one of the new photos on a page in her batik album; they have the look of happy bookends, showing that all's well, no harm done. But to me the pictures are not like that. They're documents of eternal departure.

It irks me that each of the main marks in my life, like the strata of rock that can reveal mass extinctions, is made by a man leaving. The original split, then the South America split, and now losing my father again — fresh, hurting hollows to refuse to admit. More shadow lines will appear later, traces left not by a father but by other men once I begin to look for him elsewhere. Again and again when I look down and back, what I see are these lines of extinction.

6

After my father returned to his side of the world, letters would fly across the Pacific again, now from Helen, too. That other family would become ephemeral once more; my father would sink deep. I was valedictorian at Deal that Bicentennial June and sweated through a speech in the muggy auditorium where we'd watched black girls in sequins while plaster fell on our fawn heads. And I'd keep going my old way, declining Latin nouns, drawing, turning marble: not letting the situation with the fathers leave a mark. But I'd stand before the mirror in the green cork attic, stare at my reflection, and whisper hard, *But you're pretty. And smart. And talented,* as if these words could be breathed through the glass, sink into my reflected skin.

Over the next few years my father would fly from Australia to New York or Washington once each year for diplomatic business, and Maggy and I would meet him for a weekend. His letters outlined the upcoming visit, which seemed most often spent outlining the following visit, leaving me vague and aching on the Amtrak south, staring out at the shining waters of Delaware. But Paul still came weekends for Tommy. He brought trinkets — a pen with which Nixon had signed a bill, a black penknife with the State Department seal — and he'd sit on the sofa and listen to whatever stories I told. Tales of Deal and Wilson Senior High, the wilds of black Upper Northwest. It seemed to please him that I was turning out so damned well and didn't need fancy schools like some girls. He'd shake his head, then sigh and shrug, and regard me again with eyes that lit. And it felt so thrilling and unsatisfying and dangerous and wrong to please those other girls' father. But then Tommy would skid downstairs with his backpack, Paul would get up, and they'd both say, Well, have a good weekend, and walk out the door.

When I was thirty, a woman who read my first fiction leaned across a seminar table, her eyes moist with sympathy, and said, "Girls who grow up without fathers are so full of longing."

I thought: Fuck that.

But she was right. Longing, a soft, black cavity deep at your core. And the things buried deep are the deadliest.

At fourteen, fifteen, everything felt liminal: half girl and half woman, beginning to push out the windows and doors of the house. This must be when sublimation begins, when the strange algebraic process starts whereby you start looking for your father in men, and you find or resist finding your mother in your body. This sublimation must begin when the transformation itself does. The chest, once a boy's smooth skin stretched over ribs, with two pale disks both sensitive and numb, now swells into a pair of warm, heavy, live things filling your hands. Hair sprouts between your legs, a bottom pushes at your jeans, blood's a surprise on the toilet paper; no wonder it's mostly girls in Ovid who are transfigured, becoming laurel trees, drops of myrrh, bears. This must be when the shift begins, when yearning for those pantheonic fathers who had dwelled in the ribs turns instead to men on the street, and when you might or might not become your mother.

Our house had no father but plenty of men — a big difference, because men who come to the house for your mother are like the boys who soon come for you, so you watch and learn, like it or not. A Cadillac, cab, or van would pull up to Barnaby Street every few days for a month or two or even a year, a door would crank open and slam shut, and a man would bound up the sidewalk. My mother was looking for a *mate*, she said, which as an Australian word can sound chummy and breezy but to me then was sickening and reeked of sex. The cars summed up these men. Ken arrived in a big white Lincoln with a pale leather interior, and getting in that car and being driven by him, all of us, Mom and her kids, down to the waterfront for a fish dinner at Hogate's, was a treat but felt faintly whorish. Rupert was stocky and bearded and owned a sailboat but drove a cab and was introduced as working on a book, and when we went out with him on his boat, the wind gusted, saltwater lashed our faces, and we barely made it to shore, even my mother struggling to keep her eyes bright. Bob lasted a long time and drove an old van that smelled of wet camping gear and something salty; he was another one who either owned or borrowed a sailboat, and we all went out for another day on gray water in a boat that seemed doomed. Bob is one whose tongue I saw tangle in the air with my mother's, and I had to turn away fast.

Between the more serious ones were men whose names I don't remember. One of these I met in the living room, and it was clear he wouldn't last long. While my mother was giving him a drink and talking gaily she suddenly had one of her famous coughing fits, and after gesturing with her hands for a time and trying to continue speaking, she finally flung out of the room to cough more wildly in the kitchen.

After she'd swung away through the swinging door, he turned to me and whispered, "But is she all right? Does she need help?"

I eyed him from the sofa and said, "Didn't she *tell* you about her problem?"

Sometimes, though, these men were full of promise. No, not sometimes: almost always. Whenever my mother came back from a meeting or party and said, "Oh, I've met *such* a nice *man,*" and looked off, I'd have a wild flare of hope but then at once a sickening sense that again it would all sputter and burn. If it got to the point that Maggy and Tommy and I went along on a date, that we, too, climbed into the white Cadillac and drove down to Hogate's, then there was so much hope as we walked into the restaurant with its wide windows overlooking the river, as we took our seats in a leather crescent booth. So much hope in the warm round rolls in the silver basket, the icy pats of butter, the shining blue swordfish on the wall. There might be more money. A better school. A big house in Maryland. Our mother might be happy at last. And if he didn't last forever he might at least last a while, and for a few months the sight of his car parked out front was a holiday.

Two men came close. The first was Phil, a *Post* writer we adored but who died just before my father returned to Australia, and I've decided not to put him in this book. The one who came closest after Phil was Anthony. He was tall and stately and had the look of a European from the nineteen-tens, someone you'd meet at the baths in *The Good Soldier.* His eyes seemed uncertain above his long, arched nose, his body barreled at the chest but elegant, his hair wavy and silvered. He had a splendid house and a pool in which he let us swim whenever we wanted; he let most of the neighborhood swim there, as if his house, his pool, were the local duchy and he the kind, dutiful duke. He had a sense of propriety, of graciousness; his face sometimes looked pained if the neighboring kids swam with their long, thick black hair undone and he'd need to say something about it. Once we were caught in a thunderstorm at his house and raced inside, and my clothes, left out on a lounge chair, got drenched, so he sent me up to his room, an elegant, quiet, European man's room, to find something to wear in his closet. I chose a long pink shirt with fine white ribs.

"Oh, that one I rarely wear," he said. "Please keep it."

It was soft and delicate, and buttoning it up as I stood before his big mirror, then carefully rolling the long pink sleeves above my wrists, this shirt that belonged to this fine man who seemed to love my mother in a good way and whom we wished she'd just love back, I felt covered, even more covered than you might feel after being caught in the rain and your skin's cold and damp and you slip on something warm and soft. I wore it home to Barnaby Street, took it off and hung it up, and just looked at it, this long pink shirt, the only man's shirt in the house.

What happened to Anthony I don't remember. There was always a wretched morning with my mother sitting at the kitchen table, flinging out her hand and saying, "Oh, good *riddance*." Then they just disappeared.

Aside from Anthony and Phil, the taste many of these men left in my mouth is foul. One I saw from the laundry-room window late one night when I folded towels. I watched from the basement, half underground, as he and my mother wandered up the front steps above me, the front door banged, and the stairs creaked. An hour later, he hurried out the front walk, jumped into his little sports car with his bald head and glasses, and drove off.

A house that seemed to want men, yet could or would not keep them. Girls in such a house feel men come and go like currents, feel their mother's emotion storm and subside, can't help but feel the flood on their own skin. Hope, excitement, despair, disgust. A sense of sex that is exhausting, an air of dissatisfaction.

I wonder what those girls saw of sex in their house. Maybe they seemed so interested in hearing about my mother and tormenting me about orgasms because they hadn't seen much sex in the flesh. Maybe for them it was chambered, behind the door of a bedroom down the hall: marital intimacy, a secret, a treasure. I picture it spoken of in hushed tones, drenched in mystery, requiring art.

I have a photo of Helen my father took in a castle in Austria. It's grainy and shows a dusky room, the wallpaper patterned with harlequins, the furniture scrolled, the ancient tiles dim, a Persian carpet. Helen — who's usually been the one to send pictures, tucking them in the folds of her letters — marked this sequence of photos with the names of painters they're like, and this one she called a Chardin. In it she sits at a dressing table putting up her hair, and there's a candlestick on the table, a glimpse of a baroque frame, a crucifix. My father took the photo from behind, so it shows her back, her soft, raised arms emerging from a white sleeveless blouse, her slim waist, her face reflected in the mirror. Everything about the image bespeaks treasure and value, and the image is intimate, yet composed and voluptuous; it hints at great privacy and reveals just enough.

Whereas with us, everything seemed too natural, exposed, when my mother had a new man or suddenly began cleaning in her nightie and bent over to sponge the floor, showing everything. Still, in my forties, when I look down at my naked body, it takes an effort to see myself, and not her. And a real effort to see something I like, not something artless, an emu.

Mum's the first to have been able to please Daddy, you know.

At fifteen you're sure you can get out. Out of your family, your house, out on the street, imagine you've flung off these fathers and now look at men to see how they look back.

And on the street now I was like Jenny. When I walked down Connecticut or up Western Avenue, suddenly boys' and men's eyes flashed around me, mouths murmured or shouted, horns blared. From car windows, construction sites. As if I'd suddenly stepped into view: fifteen years old, tight jeans, long blond hair. I'd walk through the light of all these eyes terrified, giddy, dazzled.

When my father returned to Australia, I hadn't been keeping a diary and didn't note it. In the diaries I'd kept as a girl, he and Paul are scarcely mentioned beyond notations that one or the other has written and I have written back; you would never know their presence or absence infused me. The diary that starts soon after my father left rarely mentions them, either. It dwells on one subject, and so does the next. They cite each kiss, each howl, each honking car, each time any man or boy looks at me, as if these books are not journals but ledgers. Proof of value, that strange thing hovering in the current between the one looked at and the one looking.

It was important to document this. In our house men were exotic, not everyday items you'd have at the table or with whom you'd fold laundry. And in my most private house when I turned fifteen, the secret house where these words were felt but not spoken, the most valuable man was the one most remote: To win him was everything. Aside from citing every glance or howl, these diaries chart, day by day for three years, the ruinous fixation I had on a boy who would not even look at me in daylight, a wild boy who was rare and cruel and came only at night. All I'd ever felt, or refused to feel, or refused to admit I felt about the fathers becomes focused, sun through a magnifying glass, on him.

Deal fed into Woodrow Wilson Senior High a few blocks up Nebraska, beyond a park called Fort Reno that had a water tower and reservoir. During the Civil War, the area had been a shantytown refuge for blacks fleeing the South, and my after-school job was to document this. The shantytown's lost now beneath the plush gardens and houses of Upper Northwest, but a hundred years later, Deal and Wilson made the place black again. To be cool then meant being black, so the white boys I hung out with gave a black lope and limp to their walk, flinging the air behind them. We smoked Kools, danced the Bump to the Brothers Johnson and Commodores and Parliament Funkadelic, and cried in falsetto voices, "*Shoo,* baby!" Some of the boys who came from black parts of D.C. or had other credentials almost passed. One had a walk and talk that made him black at a distance, until you saw his pallor and haunted blue eyes; a heroin baby, the story was, and he rarely spoke, although he sang a few words to me once as a clue. Another boy who nearly passed was three years older than the rest of us, eighteen, and he was the one I became fixed on: Sutter.

I don't remember the first time I saw him, just that one day when he looked at me I could not keep my legs moving. I'd been valedictorian at Deal, he'd soon drop out; he wore army jackets and dirty jeans and loped around the edges of Wilson. He was taller than me but slight and had a round behind like a black boy, drooping blue eyes with bruise shadows beneath them, a sweet pink mouth with a filthy Jagger tongue, a child's blond hair, rude moves. I first kissed him at my fifteenth birthday party in the basement. He had drunk seventeen beers and told someone to send me to him in the bathroom, where he stood in the dark and muttered, "Come here."

My mother never saw Sutter in daylight but knew him by the crashing in the hydrangeas at night and the bruises on my neck, and she *wished* I'd find someone who might treat me more nicely. His great-great-great-grandfather was the Sutter who'd found gold in California but died a ruin, which gave my Sutter a romantic doomed past, and he let himself be doomed, too, by dropping out, stealing cuts of steak or albums, getting fired, letting himself be beat up by a black girl, being accused of stealing things he hadn't even stolen. Sutter was the one who brought the Funkadelic and Brothers Johnson records to parties; it was understood he had kinship to blackness. It was also understood that he was king, the delinquent king, and he didn't drive, he rode shotgun.

He was elusive and famous, known to school principals, police, even to some drunk woman who careened over one night wanting a cigarette as we sat by the reservoir. She squinted in the moonlight and cried, "I know you—you're Paul Sutter!" Elusive and legendary and a perverse choice and crucial.

Gold. I pinned a "Ripley's Believe It or Not" item about the gold-mine Sutter to my cork wall. I made a list of all the songs about gold, "Heart of Gold," "Sister Goldenhair." It was significant that Sutter and I had the same last initial, so I snapped the chrome *S*'s off cars I passed walking home late at night, and poked these into my cork wall, too. I came out the heavy green doors of Wilson every day at 3:00, or cut class and came out early, or walked in the rain at night to Starvin' Steve's on Wisconsin Avenue, or roamed over the hill of Fort Reno, with one goal: to find him. Sometimes he was around and sometimes he wasn't, and even when I found him I ignored him; I had to. It was like gravity and its opposite at once: need and refusing to need. I'd spot him and turn my back, not be caught hunting. Sometimes as I sat on the wall of the horseshoe behind school, I'd see his olive-green jacket appear over the hill and I'd freeze in a panic, my lips still pulling on a Kool but frozen, my foot still kicking in a boot but frozen, as he slanted into view. If he saw me he ignored me, too. I could barely hear myself speak, could dig up nothing worth saying, nothing that would make his laughing eyes stay on me in public, although just the night before he might have thrown sticks at my window and bitten my stomach. I'd stand with my back to him, matching his cool, but my fingertip as it knocked away ash, the edge of my burning ear, knew exactly how far he was behind me, which way his crowing voice was thrown, whether the smoke from his mouth was blown in taunting rings my way. If I happened to pass into his cold, blue, laughing glance, it was enough, a silent communiqué. But then Rick's Dart would pull up, and Sutter would be the first to dive through the window, crowing at everyone ditched as the car screeched off. And even if he left silently I'd sense a lack and turn just enough to see him walking away. An old feeling, something pulled from my ribs, that pull that says the center is elsewhere, and I'd have to stand there, pretending I wasn't watching him go.

But at night I'd wait and hope and *will.* After I'd walked home dejected from wherever I'd been hunting, or burning with a truly frightening jealousy if I'd seen him glance at another girl, after I'd walked home alone in the dark, calculating the number of blocks, figuring out the hypotenuse as if there were a street at an angle instead of the numerical and alphabetical grid, reciting the names of the streets, which, this far uptown, had graduated from single letters, as streets were named downtown, to one-syllable names to two-syllable to three-, *McKinley Northampton Oliver Patterson Quesada Rittenhouse Stephenson Tennyson* and then, for no reason, *Barnaby,* once I got home and had crept past my mother's dark bedroom and gone upstairs, I'd stand at my attic window in the dark, and wait, and hope, and *will.* I'd light a cigarette and stare up at Orion, which Sutter had pointed out to me one brilliant cold night, wanting whatever else I wanted so badly but refused to want, and I'd wait, and hope, and will. Then I'd smash the cigarette out on the brick sill and flick it down into the ivy, get into bed, and wait. And if it was a lucky Friday, at 2:00 or so a car would move slowly down sleeping Barnaby Street. I'd open my eyes in the dark. A car door would creak open and a bottle would fall to the asphalt and roll to the gutter. The door would slam, the Dart would drive off, and I'd wait, not breathing, hands clenched at my stomach, until the hydrangea rustled and a bottle top pinged at my screen. Then I'd run down past my mother's bedroom in a nightie and let him in fast, and we'd creep back upstairs, past my sleeping mother, betraying and hurting and defying her at once, up to my attic, where I had a $50 stereo and would play, very low, the Stones' *Black and Blue,* which Paul Stuart had just given me for my birthday or Christmas, and Paul Sutter and I would struggle until 5:00, my underpants inched down by his fingers, my underpants yanked back up, my underpants wheedled down by his thumbs, my underpants wrenched back up, and although in my house there were no rules, my mother couldn't say much about it and there was no father to say anything, still I wouldn't let him get in those underpants and wouldn't go anywhere near his, fisted my hands and stayed away, because no matter how much I'd seen I still didn't know what to do, so we wrangled for a year and a half.

Sutter was somewhere between Peter Pan and Mick Jagger, or Pan himself — grinning, leering, feral, a creature that flies in windows at night and creeps out by daylight, can't take much daylight. He was not like Amor in Apuleius's *Golden Ass,* but that's what I was reading in Latin, so I made him Amor, too. He might have coils and scales if you turned on the light, but what you heard was the rustle at the window, a rustle of distance and night air and thrill, and what you felt was the heat of his hands and mouth wanting you. But these monster-god boys must stay exotic. They can't be homey, make polite conversation. They need to be half fantasy, unknowable, just leaving a smudge of dirt or gold on your skin as proof once they've disappeared.

———

When he'd gone I'd lie in bed and replay everything; only then, without his obliterating presence, could it become real. *Jesus*, he'd whispered, his lips at my breast. *Jesus, Jane. You.* The way he said *You.* I could still smell him — dirt and leaves and musty hair, smoky jeans and wildness; it clung to my arm, so I pressed my nose into the skin and breathed it. And the marks he left, so valuable; his eyes blurred and hungry, he'd fix his mouth to my neck and pull the blood to the surface, painful and satisfying.

He did just enough to keep me sick and craving. He called at 1:00 in the morning and whispered he was sorry to be such a bastard, wished he could be better. He scrawled that he loved me on a scrap of pink paper and left it on my desk in the dark. He gave me a snaky gold bracelet he'd probably stolen from Woodies. Once, in my room, after we'd struggled, as he sat on the edge of my bed smoking, elbows on knees and cigarette dangling from fingers, he saw where his shirt had been ripped in a fight, and pulled at the cloth slowly, let the scrap drop to the floor. It was a cotton shirt, olive with fine salmon and white stripes. I waited until he'd gone — until he suddenly jumped up and lunged down the stairs, me running behind; until, at the screen door, he kissed me hard and pulled away, out in the air now, free, already sensing the big night around him, while I stood at the door of a narrow, dark house; until he spun military on his heels and skidded down the steps, stopped to light a cigarette, flung the match into the grass, and walked with long, loping strides up the block, his shadow lengthening and shortening under the street lamp; until he turned the corner and the sound of his steps was gone and so even was the faint smell of sulfur—then I ran up to my room and snatched the piece of cloth from the carpet. I breathed it and smoothed it and put it in my diary between the pages for that day, kept it safe, like the scrawled note and snaky gold bracelet, which I put in the bar-of-gold jewelry box with the silver llama and peacock, and still have there now.

That strip of Sutter's shirt was like the pink shirt Anthony gave me the day of the thunderstorm, a shirt I would let Jenny borrow not long after putting Sutter's scrap in my book: the only other trace of a man's shirt in our house. A man's shirt was all I had that would fit Jenny when I next saw her, she was so big when she returned—because of the pill, she said, because of course she was ahead of me, always ahead of me, she'd been fucking for years. She needed a big shirt and looked in my closet until she found Anthony's, and took it off the hanger and put it on and never gave it back, and anytime I might have dreamt I was free, not thrashing against Jenny or infused with my mother or hunting my father, I was wrong.

Another thing pinned to the cork wall: a mood chart I made. It had gradations of thirty humors from *suicidal* to *ecstatic* in the left column, and a grid to the right with a square for each day. Every day I filled in a box with the dominant humor, and a red line moved from one box to the next, plunging up and down. The line rose to ecstatic three times in those years: because of Sutter and only Sutter. Not having been valedictorian at Deal, not winning the Vergil prize two years later, not getting into Princeton after that. Funny that *ecstatic* means to step out of yourself and not the reverse, to feel as complete as the little inked box.

Although I kept each scrap of Sutter in those days, I have no letters from my father, but they came. I did keep photos, or at least one of Jenny. In it she's a woman, full, her shirt tied at the waist, her hair winging back, her smile baby-sweet, although studying it I knew better. Like a stabbing needle, she could smile through that lens into my father, across the ocean, into her father, into me.

On Fridays or Sundays now her father sat and listened to my stories about Sutter, police, bricks thrown through windows — just as terrific as my prizes and jobs: the right mix. But talk always drifted like gravity to the other side of the world, to that family of such intense interest. Paul got his letters from Canberra, I got mine, and his brows rose skeptical at life glimpsed through the stationery, and he'd wonder what was *really* going on, what his girls were really up to — screwing up at school, dropping *out*? I talked to him on the phone, too, because I was the one who bolted when it rang. More and more, we talked about Jenny.

Jenny drinking and dropping out of school, Jenny in more and more trouble: men. Jenny on the horizon, laughing and knowing things, moving faster than me. But I was so smart now and hung out with those wild boys, Paul wanted to know what I thought. Maybe I could shed light on his difficult daughter.

As in his study in South America: the honor. I'd lie on the antique green-velvet sofa in my mother's room, lifting and lowering my legs as I dissected Jenny with him on the phone: her possible motives, troubles, desires. And I found myself often taking the bus down to his apartment with its white carpet, cool air, and ficus. Paul would lean back on the sofa with a scotch in his hand, and I would sit on that black leather Mies van der Rohe chair, but now I wasn't flushing and taunted, now I smoked Kools and sipped beers and wore a bomber jacket and jeans ripped at the knees to take the edge off my Vergil prize, and was very knowledgeable about self-destructive girls, and was Jenny's father's special confidante, his ally.

One of those nights, after I'd been down at Paul's and had drunk too much, as he drove me home through Rock Creek Park, something suddenly went wrong and burst, something born of the talk of that other family, caught in the choking tangles. The dark parkway, how he took the turns smoothly with one hand on the wheel, how we glided through the wet leaves, and the smell of the creek, and the moist air rushing past — out of the blue I was crying.

"He doesn't give a damn about me."

Paul looked at me fast in the darkness. "Of course he does." He might even have awkwardly patted my hand. "Of course your father loves you. He loves you *very much*." He said it so earnestly, he looked actually stricken, his face the tender face as when he once held my hand.

And later in my room, lying in bed as the green walls

spun and burning with shame that this weakness had splattered out, I wondered if downtown Paul was in his own bed, staring at the ceiling, wondering whether his own girls imagined he didn't love them: if in answering me he'd been speaking to them, looking through me again to Jenny, if, in fact, he'd always just looked through me to Jenny.

But surely he did see me. One of those summer afternoons he'd driven over not for Tommy, but for me. He came with his brother, just flown in from California. The dark red Mercedes parked out front, two tall men moving up the walk and then waiting, smiling, breathing scotch through the screen door as I opened it barefoot and wondered why they were there. They stepped inside and stood by the stairs, where my mother would let her purse drop after work.

He smiled and said he had just wanted his brother to see me, he hadn't seen me since I was eight. Paul gestured with his chin the way he'd tell me to go pose for a picture: Go stand over there.

I did.

He twirled his finger. "Go on, Jane," he said. "Turn around for us."

So I turned. Slowly, around me, the room's dark oak panels and old gold chair, then the ashy fireplace, the scrolled dining-room chairs, the brown tasseled rug, the green glowing in from the back porch, the dim kitchen. The darkness and glow revolved glassy around me, as Paul and his brother watched and appreciated. Which is what they surely did, *appreciated,* a word so full of praise and prize, they stood there and admired how well I'd turned out, how well I'd been made, as if I were Paul's and he had made me himself.

Helen's made it as if I won out as far as fathers go, leaving Jenny with none, my diary will say soon after Jenny returns. It won't react to this. It will say nothing uncertain, or sick, or despairing about one father or the other. But then, it rarely mentions them.

On Sutter, though:

I feel as though I'm beginning to split up.

Jenny did not see her father one weekend each year the way Maggy and I saw ours, because Paul did not fly to Australia. But I was sixteen and in such a hothouse I didn't care about that other side, the other story over there. I was in a hothouse that had no man, in which my mother was alone, she was the only one of them alone, and if those girls did not see their father one weekend each year, they lived with mine all the time. But mostly it was a hothouse in which I whispered at the mirror until my knuckles turned white that one father or another did not matter, whether my father loved me or knew me did not matter, the situation with the fathers did not matter, the damned fathers had left no mark on me: All that mattered was getting *out.*

Walking at dusk you get out of the house and almost out of your maddening self. Past brick houses and stirring oaks; past a single swing dropping from a tree; past a little girl on the sidewalk, dreamy, fat pink chalk gripped in each hand, drawing like swimming, turning her head and glancing up, laughing to be caught in her dream. Walking, you can disappear. You can forget your body, your head glides easy and fast, all you are is eyes, small pools lapping up what they see, pools that are permeable, you ought to be able to slip through them and into the air, into that little pink-fingered girl's laugh, up through the leaves to the constant, changing sky.

In twilit summertime Washington it was hard to see far down Barnaby Street, each oak tree more veiled by the heavy hanging air, and the asphalt gave off the day's heat as I walked barefoot, breathing hard. I'd walk three or four or ten blocks until I was empty, then sit on a curb and smoke. Or if I couldn't leave the house I'd just lean out my window, once I'd torn off the plastic and was free. The rough branches of the oaks filled the air with rustling volumes, and the cicadas' whirring and ratcheting rose and fell like waves, enough to lift you as you longed yourself out, the air a lulling temperature to let you flow like blood from your skin, out into the world and summer.

A night in our house could be like this: Tommy at Paul's, Maggy at Vassar, just my mother and me at home. Sixteen years old and forty-three, both restless. But no one was calling, the phone cord hung limp. So we sat, her on the sofa, me on the floor, near a burning lamp, playing Scrabble. We might have been eating Melting Moments she'd baked; we might have been drinking hot tea. We might have been playing our second or eighth game of the night, and in the Scrabble box lay sheets with the scores of the forty or fifty we'd played that hot month, and in my tense fingers, the pencil for scoring. The phone still had not rung, the phone would not ring, Sutter was somewhere without me. My mother didn't yet have the antique clock on the orange chest, but all the same I hear its loud ticking.

"Oh," she'd say, flicking a hand at her letters, "I have nothing worth anything. I have absolute junk. *You* probably have the *Z. And* the *X.* All I have is vowels, all *U*'s and *I*'s."

My ears would be like a cat's, my dirty foot on the floor bouncing fast, waiting, hoping to god that something would happen and I could get out. She'd scowl at her letters in their little wooden pew, and the old dishwasher would rumble and choke in the kitchen, and the telephone still hung silent and dead, and no Dart drove slowly down Barnaby Street, no van or Cadillac, either, because she'd decided she'd had enough of men, so it was the two of us in that hot house, and sweat would start sliding down the backs of my knees—but then out of nowhere her face would light, and she'd look up from her letters, look at me, beaming.

"*U*'s and *I*'s," she'd say, and break into a glorious smile. "But that's all I need, isn't it, Janie. You and I!"

And then at last a car might pull up, we'd hear it drive down Barnaby and idle. Our fingers paused above our wooden letters and words. If a bottle broke on the asphalt or a boy's voice crowed, that was it, I sprang. I had $10 in my pocket and cigarettes and was gone. Then out in the car, speeding down Utah, buying beer, until everyone was picked up.

We drove to Candy Cane City, a park with a branch of Rock Creek running through it, swingsets and slides, a field.

These outside, liminal places when you're a teenager. Ways out! At sixteen, seventeen, you shouldn't live in houses; you should hide in woods or dart in fields, move in dusk or darkness. We would roam every Friday and Saturday night outside, in winter, too, sitting in alleys to smoke and drink, climbing up the reservoir hill, staring at faraway Maryland. Candy Cane City, Dumbarton Oaks, any park anywhere, as long as it was dark, with space to run and scream. Windows broken and climbed through, girls flying from houses, boys trying to push themselves in.

Late one of those nights Sutter and I staggered drunk over the grass of Candy Cane City, and when we'd gone so far that the cars and lights of the parking lot had shrunk and all around were only dark grass, dark trees, he pulled me to the ground. His jeans smelled of soil and smoke, and the skin inside his shirt was soft. As we lay there wrangling he pushed my hand down. For the first time I let him, down over his warm belly, along the hollow of his hip, and into his jeans, into a smooth warm cave where I knew that thing was waiting, and it was, it grazed my knuckles, silky and firm like a limb.

He whispered, "Do something you've never done. *Grab* it."

I did. My head was far away, up in the night air among the ringing cicadas, and probably my eyes were shut, but when I remember this now it's as though my head and eyes were down in that cave, looking around wildly for what to do next. I held that thing in my fist, panicked, until headlights flashed on in the parking lot and shone bars of light over the grass into our eyes. I pulled my hand out fast and got up and yanked him behind me, and we went back to the others, and I could put it off again.

Why do some girls not fuck earlier? They're afraid of pain, or their virginity's precious, or they believe in some sort of love? I didn't have reasons like these. When I was six I'd been jumping on a pogo stick in the playground when the spring snapped and I fell hard and broke whatever hymen had been there. I remember lying on a table in the nurse's room, her peering between my bloodied legs and saying, "Oh, what a shame." But I like to imagine that, as an inversion of my mother's webbed platypus toes, I never had that intimate webbing: A clean, fine hole had always run through me. I wasn't afraid of being hurt; I didn't want to fuck because I had no idea how. It was too dark and confusing, so much potential to fail. Jenny had wanted me to practice with her one of those hot nights in New York; she'd rustled in the dark in her bed, moved rhythmically and sighed and moaned and finally whispered, "Come over here, Jane, and I'll show you what to do."

And I had no physical desire. Some girls at sixteen do. I'm sure Jenny did: slippery desire. I had something, an awful need in my head and chest, but this need was bony, glassy, like the numbness lodged in my ribs for so long. Or maybe that sort of desire could not be afforded, to give in would mean all those loose tubes would tumble out: got to keep everything tight. But I understood that this thing must be done sometime soon to keep Sutter, because there were so many other girls out there who roamed the land of desire.

———

Sometime after that Candy Cane night, it was decided that Jenny would come live with her father. I'm using the passive on purpose: My diary knows that Jenny decided, but there was a story, too, that my father was about to be posted again, and Jenny was too wild to go along. Once it was decided, Paul called me to discuss the new situation. He sounded sharp, alert: a situation like a mission, to rectify the previous regime's failure. I sat at the Scan desk in my mother's room, making little notes and drawings.

He couldn't understand what was the matter with Jenny. "What do you think she really wants?" he asked, and seemed really to need an answer.

"Obviously," I said, "attention."

He was silent, but I could picture his jaw tightening in his cold apartment, could see him shaking his head: If that's what she wanted, then the first thing to snap her out of this neurotic shit and get her together would be *not* to give it to her. She'd have to pick herself up by the bootstraps, like he had. The only way to learn.

He outlined a plan. She'd dropped out of school and would need her GED, and she'd sure as hell have to work. He wanted me to help her, help him straighten her out.

"Have her over, Jane. Take her out with your friends. Show her she can have it both ways, like you: You get the grades but *still know how to have fun*. I want you," he said, "to be her model."

I felt cold when he said this, and dazzled, and sick, and stared over my mother's bed into the oak trees, knowing that he knew what he said.

———

But now, anyway, there was no more time: Jenny would ask and I had to be able to shrug and say, Sure. It happened on the screened porch that hung beneath my mother's bedroom and on whose roof she sometimes sunned. The porch pushed out into the trees, a screened cube surrounded by screeching cicadas and oak leaves so dense they made the air like green flesh. That's where I did it, on a yellow lounge chair — the chair that wasn't stolen from the terra-cotta balcony in South America, the surviving one. But because the chair that was stolen was what betrayed Paul and, in a way, spirited us manless to Washington, I see the lounge chair on which I lay that night, June 17, six years after the plumbers broke into Watergate, with my pants pulled off and the weave of the plastic cushion pressing into my skin, as the same chair that was stolen, a magic chaise longue that had flown off the porch and taken me with it and settled me on the porch on Barnaby, at 2:00 in the morning, with Sutter pushing naked on top of me, and my mother, through the porch roof, sleeping or longing above us.

"Stop thinking about your mother," he whispered, after he let my breast loose from his mouth and sank his face in my hair. "You think too damn much about your mother."

7

When Jenny reached Washington, she was seventeen and Barnaby Street rang with cicadas: the ones that crawl from the ground every seventeen or thirteen years, or the ones that emerge each summer. *Magicicada,* order Lepidoptera. They clung to the crocodile hides of oak trees, buzzed through the filmy air, whirred and ratcheted their tiny tymbales. They left on the sidewalks their crumpled glassy shells, iridescent and golden, dry legs curled up. For seventeen or thirteen or a single year they'd been larval, underground, eating and forming bodies: thoraxes thickening, wings growing glossy on a fine network of veins, membranes turning to sheaths they shed one after the other. But you don't see this. It's their ringing and shells you know. After all that time underground, the cicada itself — grown nymph encased in ephemeral shell — finally cracks out and flies into the air, becomes sound.

Birds and sea turtles leave their shells when they're born; molluscs and snails leave theirs when they die. What we have for shells: first our mothers, maybe, and then our own skins.

The house on Barnaby Street became porous that summer after the night on the lounge chair, only gritty screens between us and the world. Sutter whistled low and threw bottle caps or climbed in the basement window, landed on the tiled floor, crept in stinking sneakers upstairs. We broke a pane in the basement door to get in down there, where no one would hear. My mother climbed out her bedroom window onto the porch roof to sun, her bikinied body as it was in those slides my father had shot a mile away, thirteen years earlier. I leaned out my window at night and smoked, flicked the cigarette against Miss Blaine's brick wall so that it scattered orange sparks in the darkness. A bat flew through that window: a rustle, then a dark form flitted between my face and the book at my knees, *The Other*.

Inside, the house was porous, too. The phone upstairs lived in my mother's room, so when I came home late without Sutter, I crept in as she slept or tried to sleep on that ancient, spoiled mattress, and dragged the phone as far as its cord could reach up my attic stairs. But when I came home with him, we fucked in my room and then lay there, and smoke drifted from the crack beneath my door and through the crack beneath her door as she lay alone, just as it had crept under my door in Canberra when she and the rest were on the other side. Sutter sat on my bed in the dark, and I watched the burning glow move toward his mouth, flare briefly and drop, leaving a bright trail of orange that lingered.

Once he'd left, I turned on the lamp and drew on the calendar a tiny circle with a dot at its center: sex. Then I registered the day's humor on the long, gridded chart, and because he'd just been there, *Happy*. The next morning, when it was safe to pluck the diaphragm out, I'd bring to the bathroom a glass slide and drip on it a dangle of his slippery stuff, press another slide on top, and hurry with this tucked in a sleeve to my room and sit at the desk, look at the slide under the microscope, and study the blur for tiny homunculi, miniature relics of Sutter.

So by the time Jenny arrived, I could just say, Of course. She came in June or July or August, my diary doesn't note when; her name just starts appearing as often as Sutter's, although it's true he is often just *he* or *you*. *I love you, I hate you, I cannot stand this, where are you!* Before Jenny came my mother and Tommy and I must have sat at the yellow kitchen table and talked about her, because Jenny was Tommy's sister, after all, coming to live near him for the first time in his life. What did she want, what would she get. Her coming to Washington was surely an act of will, a plan, like that first time the girls sent Paul their live voices, like that first time they called us and asked us their strange questions, like her pulling me through a door in New York, a door I'd never even seen but that she opened like parting the wall itself, and pulled me into a hot, painted stairwell that was nowhere, where we crouched and whispered and smoked. Her head glided forward, eyes open, looking. Thirteen years, seventeen years: Surely she was coming for something.

I picture her flying over the Pacific, watching the plane's tiny shadow flit upon the crinkled sea. Maybe she thought about time zones, like I would, and drew charts on the Qantas napkin to figure out where each zone changed, what time it truly was just then in her pocket of air. But maybe she didn't look out the window, was not transported to see the undersides of clouds. *I'm just telling you one thing. Don't ever leave yourself behind.*

Whenever she arrived, there was a day when Paul invited me down for lunch and a swim. Jenny had moved into his study and scattered her things all over his desk. Her hair was dark and coiffed, and she was heavier, eyes bright, breasts enormous.

"It's the pill," she said, as we put on our swimsuits. She looked down at her breasts, took them in her hands and shook them, then gazed over at mine and grinned. "Yeah, Mum told me I'd be the only one like this around you all."

On the hot, bright roof we swam, I smoked, my hair caught in the flame, and Jenny brushed the sizzled strand away. "Hang on," she said, "I'll have one, too," and she groped in the immense bag she carried everywhere, lipsticks, gum, brushes, postcards, lighters, tampons, tarot cards, pens.

"So?" I said, after she'd exhaled in a rush and gazed out at Washington stretching hazy around us.

"So," she said. "Here I bloody am."

She told me about her boyfriend in Canberra, and school, and the end of it, and the speed and the cars and the dope and the flats and the dole of Australia. "Pissants," she said. "Waste of time. But oh! What will I do without him?" She wriggled and kissed a picture of her boy.

"So you didn't want to leave?"

She looked away. "Of course I did."

"Why?"

But she just gazed privately out at the city, white light glowing around her dark hair.

I worked evenings serving dinner to a house of Jesuits but had the days free, so for the next few weeks I'd take the bus downtown and get Jenny, and we'd swim, wander, go to museums. She wore long loose men's shirts, tight leggings, and pointed shoes with stiletto heels that dug into the floor or struck the sidewalk with metal; she carried that purse of junk everywhere. She was never ready, so in her bathroom, Paul's bathroom, I'd sit on the rim of the tub and watch her put on eyeliner and spray her hair and stroke red lipstick on her baby-sweet mouth, smiling at herself and at me in the mirror amid cans of spray, bottles of gel, tubes and boxes of lipstick, cream, and powder, their gold and silver labels all around her reflected self. Hair spray hung in the air with the smoke curling up from the cigarette she'd set burning on the edge of the sink. If Paul was home his mouth would tighten; he'd move through the apartment shaking his head at the new stains on the rug, ashes on the table, piles of dishes and trash in the kitchen, preposterous mess in the spare bathroom, general aimlessness of Jenny, because from the start it was not clear what she wanted.

We wandered down Eighteenth Street. Jenny kicked her feet out, her black shoes with nasty heels landing on the concrete hard, her face high and eyes challenging. We sat for a cigarette on the edge of a monument, at a horse's bronze hooves, and I said what was expected: Why hadn't she just finished high school, she should have at least gotten a diploma, she was stupid, that was a mistake. She half listened, grew fey, blew smoke rings, laughed, crossed her legs and tossed her foot up and down in annoyance, jumped up to keep walking, slipped into her own private zone away from me, and her father, and the whole bloody world.

We walked on through the muggy air. The glaring Mall, the Museum of Natural History. Only in that echoing, cool space, that underwater light, did she seem to move in her medium. She gazed up at the huge blue whale suspended from the ceiling and reached to stroke its sleek skin, as if the whale and its underwater ilk were the only ones who knew her, and I turned away and saw again her blood on the sand, on the marble floor. Then her soft private sighs could go on for blocks as we walked back to Paul's, and even though I'd resolved not to, I couldn't help it and finally said, "*What?*"

She gave a little laugh and pulled herself up from the depths. "Oh," she said, shrugging. But once more let her eyes wander toward the private world she seemed to try to make valuable by making private, smoke drifting as if forgotten from her lips.

Back at Paul's, I'd fall upon the sofa while she slid a cassette in his player, something I had to hear, she couldn't believe I didn't know it already. *You had a temper, like my jealousy* . . . I sat across from her as she sang, eyes shut, mouth a small *O*, and even if I wanted to listen I couldn't, I wouldn't, everything about her made me clamp shut.

My glass neatly centered on the coaster was not like Jenny's sweating on the table; my ashes tapped cleanly into the ashtray were not like hers melting in watery rings; my boy-jeaned legs were not like Jenny's carefully torn stockings. My body went stiff, every movement watched by Jenny, whose every movement was watched by me. And on played her songs through those stupefying afternoons, air heavy and green and full of whales' cries, perpetually underwater.

I'm coming back love, cruel Heathcliff . . .

But then a key would turn in the lock and there was Paul, the air clarifying around him. He stood in the doorway with his polished shoes, hand fisted at hip. He looked at the appalling state of the apartment, breakfast dishes still on the counter, milk sitting out, wrappers and records and cigarettes and shoes and things from that goddamned *bag* all over. He looked at Jenny, who did not even open her eyes but sang more sweetly, raising her chin, showing her white neck, pouting her stained lips to the far crying of whales.

Four fast steps to the stereo and it was switched off. In the new silence Jenny smiled, as if with fresh pleasure in being denied. When he jingled his keys and nodded at me to say he'd drive me home, Jenny rose, too. A curt shake of the head: no. So she smiled again, as if more deeply satisfied because more deeply denied, dropped her bag on the sofa, dropped herself, too. His hand at my back, Paul maneuvered me courtly through the door, and Jenny, her mouth in its private curling smile, pulled from her bag a pen and cards and began to write, smoke drifting from her nostrils.

"So what do you think," he'd ask in the Mercedes as we rushed beneath the leaves.

When you're sixteen or seventeen meaning can be anywhere. A drop of rain running down the window is a symbol, a song comes on the radio just when you longed for it, you have the same initials as the boy for whom you're sick, secret messages await you in poems. It's like living in a net of logic, of systems of words and significance. The number of words was finite, I thought, and all knowledge was contained in words, so it must be possible to have complete knowledge, if only you had the capacity. Time was always ticking by, I thought, which meant numbers floated in the air like molecules, so if they could enter your pores you'd be precisely conscious of time, if you only had the capacity. It was a matter of letting logical matter seep into your skin. Stories, myths, lyrics of songs had codified human patterns, and you just had to find the one that applied to you. *The master plan,* said spooky boys: traces of the overriding logic found everywhere from license plate numbers to a sequence of songs. And dreams, of course; dreams told you everything. In that subliminal land you got clues to what would happen next. It was all plotted out: You just had to step along the path made for you, like Cassandra toward the blood in the bath.

A month of hot days downtown as Jenny brooded and smoked and haunted her diary, as heat lightning flashed between her and Paul; a month of solitaire on the floating back porch and making dinner for the Jesuits. Somewhere up the coast at a Jersey beach was Sutter, so there was no tapping at my window at night, no rustling in the hydrangeas. A letter came: scrawled block print, words spelled wrong, fragments of songs that then played in my head. *Me and Crazy Janie were making love in the dirt, singing our birthday songs...*

Then a few hundred Atlantic miles south of Sutter, we went to the beach, too: Paul invited me along. It was my beach, so why shouldn't I go. Besides, I was needed as aide-de-camp. *Paul and Jenny have never really been together in a father-daughter atmosphere . . . And I know how hard it will be for the two of them to discuss things . . . God, I'm glad I'm not really in all this.*

I had my learner's permit, and Paul said he'd teach me to drive a stick shift. So one afternoon at the beach, in the hot slanting light, the air humming with gnats, he came out the screen door in his flip-flops and tossed me the keys to his convertible. "Here," he said, his face the same tender face with sky behind it as when he once held my hand. "Here you go, Jane. Get on in."

Jenny came out, too, trussed up to strut the boardwalk. The three of us stood a moment outside the house by the dark red Mercedes, the grass tough, asphalt hot, cicadas whirring in the pines. She shook her bracelets and stepped forward in her wicked shoes, reached for the door, she wanted to drive, too, but Paul shook his head. He stepped forward to block her and opened the door for me to get in. So I did get in, and put the key in the ignition and shifted as Paul showed me. The car jolted to life, and Paul and I drove toward the shore, in the lowering sun, leaving Jenny laughing and humiliated on the grass. Just as she once drove off with my father, with her conquering slit foot, while I stood behind mute and ruined.

That was when she wrote that diary entry or note, at the same beach where years before I'd nearly drowned.

*I'm just telling you one thing. Don't ever leave yourself be-
hind . . . you've got to know where the hell you're going and
why. Otherwise — once you get there — you won't really
know why the hell you're there . . .*

You'll find that you've left yourself behind . . .

*Actually — the truth is that I'm bullshitting. What
you've really got to do is find yourself again — because you
lose yourself in the process — somewhere in the middle of the
Pacific or something.*

Back in Washington she came to stay at Barnaby Street, where
my mother suddenly got to be hostess and show her real
self after all those years. She clasped Jenny's hands, looked
searchingly into her eyes, sat her down at the table, maybe
baked Melting Moments or Afghans, made evident in an instant, I thought, that she could never have been the one to
do it first. Up in my room Jenny bounced on both twin beds.
She sat at my desk and touched the chrome *S*'s jabbed in the
cork, the "Believe It or Not" about Sutter's gold, the calendar
with its secret codes, then smiled and turned away.

Sutter was still gone, but other boys would pull up at
night. She'd quicken, ready to go, who cared where.

"This is my stepsister," I'd say as we climbed into a Dart.
"My stepsister Jenny."

"Stepsister!" she cried, her Aussie voice exotic. "Must you
say that? I feel like something disgusting — with warts!" She
laughed and leaned toward the front seat. "But the fact of
the matter is," she whispered, "next to Jane, of course, I *am*
wicked."

Her big, loose shirt was open low so breasts swelled forward trimmed in lace, necklaces lost in between, eyes of Alan and Jimmy lost there, too. At parties she sat alone and drank red wine and wrote poetry in the dark. She'd pull scraps of paper from her bag and write, smiling to herself and smoking — letters to her boy in Australia, poems, poems that were letters, diary entries. She'd get up and come over in her leggings and pointed heels and kneel at my feet, give me a poem in her curlicue writing, poems of velvet and blood. I could not read these poems, could not stand to hear them.

"We're fairytale sisters," she'd whisper. "Snow White and Rose Red. We're bound together."

She'd take my face in her hands, gaze into my eyes, and kiss me, while across the room the boys elbowed each other and laughed. Then she'd stand up, cock her hip, and go kiss one of them, too.

"Your sister's wild," the boys said.

"Stepsister."

"She seemed," one of those men told me recently, "mostly she seemed very angry. At you."

"She seemed," another friend told me, "she seemed like a darker version of you."

"That's silly," said my mother. "You're not even related."

Systems of thought when we were younger, lying hot in her pink room: nomenclatures and charts, static. The periodic table, families and orders of insects, names of who begat whom after Chaos or Nothingness. Collections of bare knowledge, not anything we yet lived. But now, at sixteen and seventeen, we replaced these static systems with others that followed logical narrative paths, paths we must follow ourselves.

I like that a larval cicada is called a nymph, because the ethereal word is so wrong for a moist, maggoty thing. The naming itself is sublimation: transforming the base to the lofty. A nymph will shed five glassy skins before emerging as an adult, then has six weeks to sing, mate, and die. *Nymph, imago, metamorphosis*: The language of entomology nears that of myth, where human patterns and transformations are codified, especially the interesting ones where something has gone wrong. A girl who cannot bear to be touched turns into a tree, virginal, evergreen. A girl who is worth nothing and has nothing to say becomes a cave and an echo. A girl who refuses to love or be loved is turned into stone. The stories of families are more complex and need phases, often spring from an original curse or crime. It can take a generation for the crime to be avenged or the curse like poison to work its way through the bloodline. A girl is sacrificed by her father, so her mother must kill him, and then the mother's son must kill her, so he, too, must be killed . . . Logical compulsion, psychological compulsion. A girl is abandoned by her father, so she must steal someone else's. These compulsions are like secret rivers running through your brain. You must play out again and again the prime event, to make it turn out right, or make sure you are perpetually ruined so the narrative itself is intact. These channels run through you but encase you, too, as if you are an oyster, nymph, or tree and keep putting out the same shell, a shell patterned by your growing: the glassy shell that is your natural form, out of which you want to smash free.

Jenny flew over the Pacific with a bag full of meaningful music, fairy tales, tarot cards, poems, and, deep inside, her secret, black, precious possession: the split sparkling like a geode. Smoking at her father's desk, she turned her tarot cards over and over, and maybe she found predetermination each time. We're Snow White and Rose Red, she'd say again and again, and look at me emblazoned with meaning. But I didn't know the story and didn't want to. *God, I'm glad I'm not really in all this.* She'd look at me bemused then, as if marveling that I would not understand the simple systems that impelled her.

> *The two children loved each other so dearly that they always walked hand in hand when they went out together, and when Snow White said, "We will never separate from each other," Rose Red replied, "Not so long as we live!" And their mother said, "What each girl has, she must share with the other."*

Sure enough, the main thing the two girls would share was a wild bear that was no bear at all but a hidden prince dressed in gold.

And sure enough, for the first time in our lives we'd be together on our birthday. Two years after the famous party when Sutter had whispered, *Come here.*

By then, Jenny had a job at a purse store downtown. For my seventeenth, her eighteenth, birthday, she gave me a bag from that store, a dark red leather, crescent-shaped bag with a brass zipper, which I hated. Pictures show the presenting of gifts, in her father's apartment. Paul's mother, Elsie, was visiting from Los Angeles, and Tommy was there, too, so there were lots of people for Jenny and me to share. In one photo, we kneel side by side on Paul's deep white carpet, Jenny dark haired in a man's pearly shirt and black vest; me in a mauve blouse, flushing and blond. Snow White, Rose Red. In another picture I pull the wine-dark purse from its wrapping as Jenny smokes and smiles and watches me, as we'd decided to exchange presents at Paul's and not at my party the night before.

At that party we'd drunk a lot making dinner, drunk a lot more after that, drunk until everything had bounced and melted. Sutter kept not being there, not at 8:00 and not 9:00 and not even at 10:00, Sutter, my prize, my gold. I kept glancing toward the door, pretending I wasn't, glancing out the window, looking away, drinking more. When a car pulled up and he finally came, he staggered, bleary, and fell into the gold chair: my punishment for having dared claim him. A single instant is frozen then: As I step toward him in his gold chair one of the boys, laughing, steers me away, because Jenny steps toward him as well. Then there was a jumble, we piled into cars and went to another party, but I lost her then, it was too hard to keep track. And I lost Sutter, too, just plunged into the music and smoke and beery mud. Hours later the springs in my other twin bed squeaked when Jenny finally came home.

What I would learn the next day, two hours after pulling that purse from Jenny's wrapping as she smiled and watched me, an hour after Paul had driven me home through Rock Creek Park, was that when I lost Jenny she'd been where you'd expect: fucking Sutter in the hydrangeas.

What her father said to her then I don't know. Did he call her a whore, ask how the hell she could have done something so disgusting to *Jane,* of all people?

I myself was cold and shrugged. Nothing had hurt me. Nothing like that could possibly hurt me. I had her stay over a week later to prove it, and while there she hunted through my room and read my diary, to see what I really thought.

But I doubt she found in that book what she wanted, because Jenny never seemed to get what she wanted, and that diary doesn't even give me what I want now.

It doesn't, for instance, report what I did when I learned about Sutter and Jenny, after her father had driven me home and the *love-the-one-you're-with* boy called to tell me what had happened. I went up to my room, stood before the mirror in the dark, stared at myself gasping in the glass, and said, *But you're pretty. And you're smart. And you can draw. And you smoke! And you drink! And you fuck!* Then I hit myself in the face, one cheek and then the other, and did it again, and again, my head jerking back.

Downtown, Jenny — not that night but soon after — took a bottle of scotch from her father's liquor cabinet and a knife or a blade and went into the bathroom and cut her wrists. Or maybe just one wrist, but enough to spill blood all over his tiles, enough to make her black out on the floor. I think Tommy found her.

Paul drove her to George Washington Hospital, then called us. (*I feel guilty because I feel I should. But I don't really. I don't know. Numbness.*) I remember phone calls all day, nets across the ocean: health insurance, legalities, the prospect of plane tickets proposed, then abandoned, whose fault this bloody well was. At some point my father and Helen called me.

It was of tremendous importance that I go to see Jenny, my father said on the phone. Of tremendous importance to her and her mother. I may not know it, they said, but I mattered a great deal to Jenny. She loved me very, very much. So they hoped I would visit her often, please, while she was mending in the hospital.

So I did. I took the bus down to Washington Circle after school on Fridays and went up to the psychiatric ward on the sixth or seventh floor. Jenny seemed happy to see me. She seemed almost proud of the place, her new, shining territory in the sky. She strutted before me down the bright hall, swinging her bandaged wrist and silver slave bracelet as she pointed out the television room and blew kisses at the lunatics. In her room, she sat on the bed, I sat on a chair, and we looked at each other, her with a bag full of poems and garbage and me with a bag full of Latin and math. She smiled and suddenly grabbed my hand, kissed it, and swore that fucking Sutter had not meant a thing.

"Just call me a whore," she said. "*Come* on. Call me a whore and then we'll be even. I don't think he even *came*. I know I didn't."

I could say I was drunk, Sutter told me later. *Or that I didn't know what I was doing, I lost my head, I'm sorry, but they're all just excuses. I could also say I was seduced.*

"Oh *come* on, Jane!" She looked at me with those eyes hot and live and dug her nails into my wrist. "Don't be such a condemning bitch. Just say it!"

But I wouldn't, so after a while she turned away. Then smiled her dreamy smile and hummed and blew her dreamy smoke rings.

Of course she smiled, because she'd won. Telephones ringing across the oceans, both fathers, both mothers, intent upon her, Sutter stolen with ease. She'd won everything.

And no one noticed, because they were laughably minor, that I had little scars on my wrists, too. After I'd learned what she and Sutter had done, after slapping myself in the face, I'd gone down to the bathroom and tried cutting my own wrists, but not with a knife because I was not as strong as Jenny. Instead, with the small, sharp prongs of the metal clasp that binds an Ace bandage. I found the bandage in the bathroom cabinet, unwound it, took the metal clasp, washed it with hot water and soap, and pressed the prongs into my wrist to make two little vampire holes. I pulled the prongs across the thin, green veins, enough to fray the skin, but I just could not push harder; it hurt. So after trying a few times I washed the claw and hooked it back in the bandage, put it in the cabinet, turned off the light, and went upstairs.

In my green bedroom, at the balsa desk, I took out my microscope and placed Jenny under the lens. I laid her down gently and pressed pins through her hands and feet. Then I took the scalpel from my blue plastic dissecting kit and cut a careful slice from her haughty neck, between her breasts, and over her soft, blue stomach to that part of her I don't recall ever seeing although I must have, first a bare little peach in the bathtub in Canberra and then more like a mouse in her bathroom in New York, a part that Sutter, anyway, must have seen and wanted. I drew a knife down to that spot and peeled her skin carefully apart and pinned it to either side of the board and examined what I found inside.

> She's sure she isn't really bad . . . She wants to prove me not as good as Paul Stuart has always built me up to be as her model. I don't know how much the whole family history has to do with it. Helen's made it as if I won out as far as fathers go, leaving Jenny with none. But I really don't think that's affected her much — it hasn't me . . .

When Jenny was released from the hospital she returned to her father's study for a time and got a job at the Smithsonian museum shop. That Christmas, she gave me two books: a catalog of fantasy illustration and a Smithsonian diary (*For Jane Alison Stuart. Christmas, 1978. With love, Jenny Cummins*). She took the first five pages with a poem she'd written called "Realizations." After it she added a note:

> Jane — do you remember the excerpt I read you from my diary. I had written it the night I slit my wrist — it talked of my outside. I thought, at the time, that I could find it through death. But, I had forgotten this poem, which really is true. I cannot find my outside through death. I cannot

even look for it. It cannot be found. So I will never again re-
peat my act of Nov. 24. Anyway — how could I have been so
selfish as to deprive the world of me — or to deprive myself of
those I love — like you Jane. With much love, Jenny C. T. G.

Insides and outsides. A girl standing before a mirror with lipstick in her hand, making herself up for someone; a girl standing before a mirror with a knife in her hand, breaking herself for someone. The image you see in the glass does not accord with the vaporous thing inside you that sees. The vaporous one is made of words that keep flowing along paths, the same stream of thoughts and impulses. When I was nine I'd once looked at my hand on a tree trunk in South America and marveled that inside the skin flowed consciousness and *me*; it was a miracle to be conscious. Now the idea of consciousness in skin was suffocating, the same blood moving around and around in this membrane: I wanted to cut it open to let the poison out. Bloodletting, humors. But I couldn't do it then and can't now; it hurts.

Jenny could. Cutting her wrist in the bathroom: She wanted to find her outside. Which means she wanted to find the hard, pretty girl in the mirror, finally be that thing that looked so valuable but kept being worthless? Or to get outside, out of her skin? That unhappy, pressing a sharp blade into your wrist, feeling the skin split, watching the blood trickle, pressing deeper — that unhappy, you surely want to escape. Your self is not at home inside you but at large, longing for an ancient center that's lost: a ghost in exile inside its own flesh.

———

When Jenny came down from the sixth or seventh floor, it might have seemed that a crisis had passed, she'd done what she needed and this battle could finally end. In one of the *Anne of Green Gables* books, a child ponders the word *crisis*. But she confuses it with *chrysalis,* which means golden sheath and denotes a state through which a larva passes before metamorphosing into an imago, the final perfect form of the insect. But imago also means, psychologically, an idealized image of a parent that a child forms and cannot be free of, an image that persists as the child grows old. Had Jenny done as she needed her mother to have done, taken the man at the party? I'd done as I feared my mother had, lost the man at the party, just could not hold on to him.

But, of course, I'd already taken Jenny's. Which even now I'd probably do once more if I were four or eleven and the split happened again.

Jenny said she'd never again do what she did, but she was wrong. Again and again she'd stand before a mirror with a knife. But there are other ways to get out. What I did was drink. She'd cut; I'd black out. The first time, sixteen, I drank a bottle of kirsch and disappeared easily, became someone else who did not talk or walk like me and did things I would never do, and I remembered none of it. One of the boys sang a song to me outside Wilson later to narrate what I'd done. When he did, a black hole opened up, panic at having no memory, as if for a time I'd been extinct. But, I decided, as I hurried hot down Fessenden Street to the bus stop, clamping Apuleius to my chest, since I had no memory of what I'd done, I hadn't really been there. So I hadn't actually done it; it wasn't me; it was someone else. Which meant I could do it, and therefore not do it, again.

I'm glad I'm not really in this . . . The family history hasn't affected me much . . . Amnesia and suppression, a black hole in the brain. Whereas Jenny, as always, was ahead, slicing herself open and peering inside.

That fall she wrote a poem for me, and maybe she read it aloud one of those nights, but if so, I didn't listen. I didn't see the poem for years. In it she examines me, as I'd dissected her, as she'd peered into herself. She sees something I've buried deep and keep in darkness, she writes, something I've locked inside and can't reason with or make go away.

> *Stay as you are Jane —*
> *But I will come*
> *Soon I will come*
> *And dig it out of you . . .*

What she'll dig out, she says, what she'll pry from my depths, will be ugly and frightening. And when she digs it out, it will envelop me as I stand unaware, vulnerable for the first time. This thing she'll pry out, that I'm afraid of, is *Love.*

Amnesia evidently can coexist with a craving to know everything, to catch all the words and numbers afloat in the air. Maybe the two are necessary correlatives, or maybe all those logical particles can collapse into atoms and break down to oblivion. I wrote an essay about the concept of omniscience on the emu-and-kangaroo letterhead my father had given me, and got into Princeton the spring after Jenny came. But Princeton had a policy concerning financial aid, which I needed badly: Both parents, if divorced, had to file a statement. Former stepfathers didn't, though. In his memoir, Geoffrey Wolff describes how furiously his father reacted to this policy. Mine did the same in a letter, with one from Helen, which I did not keep but that my diary tells me *flatly refused tuition money and was intended to make me (us) feel guilty . . . For never attempting to visit him? For allegedly throwing Helen into a terrible financial situation?* — letters that made that diary of mine finally explode at the situation with the fathers.

Just before leaving for Princeton, I dreamt I was in my mother's bed with a friend's father. *There were two of me, one physical . . . the other, seeing and thinking everything, was a little below and a little beyond . . . So he started making love to me, but he was talking very concernedly and businesslike the whole time. It was no fun. Then suddenly she came home, so we had to rush. It was awful. Putting on clothes, etc. I felt so guilty, but then it was sort of my father, and I thought everyone goes to bed with their fathers! Some, in fact most, of this is traceable. I'm not going to bother writing it.*

I just realized that I'm alone and myself — the same as in the mirror. And right now I wish I weren't.

8

⌒⌒

There's so often a hole at the heart of first-person narratives: a black hole like the windy center of consciousness, or like Odysseus calling himself *No One* in the Cyclops's cave. The self seems so nebulous: What's it made of? Paths of words that follow obsessive patterns, images that rise and sink again, repetitive ways of doing things. There must be a fixed number of all these, so the self should be finite and recognizable. Then why does it seem so vaporous, no more certain than weather? The grammatical construct itself implies clarity: I am this, I am that. Yet the verb *to be* denotes a falsity, because what precisely equals anything else or stays in a fixed condition? And the subject — I: how could such a slight figure denote the rushing, shifting, remembering, forgetting, multiplying nonsubstance in the skin?

Ovid gave these ideas such beautiful flesh: Bodies change and are permeable; the self is unfixed. All breath and words, it slips through our openings; it enters, exits, can be lost.

Just as there can be a hole in these narratives, a memoir can be as much about what's forgotten as what's remembered.

When I was nineteen, twenty, I seemed to have an alternate self that lived away from my consciousness, wanting and doing things I couldn't believe I'd do and refused to remember. Like an Ovidian figure of Hunger or Greed, climbing out night after night and leaving me wrecked.

Ways out. Jenny did work at the Smithsonian for a time, and at a local college she studied poetry, chemistry, oceanography, but before long I was told that she cut her wrists again; sometime later, her neck. A Renaissance painting shows a martyred saint being buried. Because the saint had been beheaded, her kind buriers placed her head back where it belonged, a fine red line ringing her neck. Jenny didn't die when she cut her neck; I think she just looked again and again at the idea of dying and left traces of that looking on her skin. She became attached to a skull she named Clarence or Herbert and kept on her father's desk, with candles like Mary Magdalene: *memento mori*. Remember, remember, even while you push into the black to forget. For a time she lived in a studio Paul owned in Foggy Bottom, until Maggy, returning from Vassar, moved in. Where Jenny went after that I'm not sure — here and there with her bag, on the floors of friends.

Whereas I went to Princeton: the princess and the witch. Although in each of us was a portion of the other. Her Romantic poets, my Horace and Ovid; her poems, my drawings; we both studied oceanography, we both loved the sea. I went to Princeton because of *This Side of Paradise*. Reading Fitzgerald one night when I was fifteen I'd suddenly realized that reading would always pull me out and away. Fitzgerald's world still lingered in the slate paths and magnolias of

Princeton, in the air of the young people muddy fresh from the playing fields and lakes. When I got there I didn't know what eating clubs or prep schools were and had never seen so many white people in one place, never so many white men. I wore a paper apron and served them ziti and baked chicken at Commons, part of my scholarship deal, together with loans, working summers, and all my mother put in. I stayed away from the clubs that had tormented Fitzgerald, joined a benign one, and later ran the parties there. And did well enough, publishing drawings in the *Nassau Lit*, winning a prize to study in Italy. This was the bright, formal information that appeared in letters to my father and Paul.

Paul seemed impressed by his demistepdaughter at Princeton on scholarship and sent me $100 a month for a time (not, he said, to buy fancy cars, or form expensive drug habits, or indulge in blackjack in Atlantic City, or play the stock market: *This money is for pizza and beer! Love Paul*). He visited once on his way somewhere, and I was supposed to see him again before he headed home, but didn't; I couldn't get out of bed. He waited downstairs in the dark, woody lounge and after an hour or so left a note on a scrap he found on the coffee table. I don't know if he turned the paper over and saw what had been written on the other side, or if he'd even chosen that scrap because of it. In red marker, by a man in the band that had played at the party:

Jane:
sparkles on her eyes
no spontaneity
likes dancing

20 years old
from W DC
mixed-up childhood
nice perfume
forgets what she's talking about
then denies it.
~~fish net~~ horizontal rib stockings nice
legs

I remember sitting in the library of the club with the band, legs up on the table, mirrors, cocaine, but I don't remember this man making his list. Or another man or maybe three who had left me in that same room at dawn a week earlier, left me slumped on a red leather chair with no pants on, no underpants, no memory; or any of the other men like them over those years. I'd found another boy to adore, another hard, cold boy who'd have nothing to do with me, and I'd follow him helplessly from party to party. Then give up, black out, two or three times a week, fuck whoever I'd been talking to when I blacked out, remember nothing, just wake up on a wet lacrosse field, naked, with cuts on my back, or suddenly come to myself crying on Prospect Street at 4:00 in the morning, running home barefoot on ice. Everything I didn't remember would be so ruining that I'd lock the door, go straight to my desk and Oxford editions of Ovid or Plato, and translate, look up hundred of words, try to memorize them, mark with an angry dot each word in the dictionary I'd failed to memorize as a record of my stupidity, do nothing but translate black lines of Horace or Homer on hot white pages until finally I couldn't stand the burning lamp or damned verb endings or myself anymore and went out and blacked out again.

I wouldn't stop drinking until I'd transformed. Hesiod warns men not to bathe in the water a woman has touched because it's filthy; and nasty stuff slides out when Pandora opens her box or jar or own personal self; and Plato tells a story about a hungry female named Lack who rapes a self-contained male named Wealth; and I became fixated on the repulsive female part of the sexual equation, on orifices, on need. The whole sexual arrangement seemed economic, pure intake on one side and output on the other, and the female portion felt like nothing but need. Economics from *oikos,* house. I would see Barnaby Street and my mother holding a glass of wine and a chicken leg and saying she just needed a *man,* and I'd feel my skin, my organs, actually harden. I'd refuse to need a thing, was disgusted by even having a mouth, wouldn't eat, refused to feel. But after a while the petrifaction began to force that jagged hollow inside to explode. When it was unbearable I would rush out the door to anywhere else, anywhere but my own room and skin. As fast as I could I was gone, and the other thing that was nothing but mouth and need took over again.

Fucking on tables or bathroom floors, in cars on the New Jersey Turnpike; spewing a language, I'd be told, that wasn't English or Spanish, Latin or Greek; waking up naked and choking, mouth full of water, in a pool. And when I woke up in my bed, clothes and ruin all around, I'd get out of that place of dissolution fast and hurry to shake the sheets, fold them, smooth them, pretend some unknown thing hadn't slid between me earlier and me then. Sick as I served chicken steaks to football players in Commons, I'd keep my head down and look for clues to what I'd done, with which of them. Beyond what I'd already found in the morning, the bruises and scratches on my breasts, the mess between my legs. And because someone who erupts each night but refuses to know she wants anyone to touch her isn't likely to shove in a diaphragm, there was that to worry about, too.

I've been drunk every night for almost three weeks. Everything's changed, everything and every word I used to be able to use to describe myself. I don't know when I lost myself... I can't talk to anyone about this because I'm so ashamed. If how I act when I'm drunk is how I really am then I hate myself.

This other person, this craving thing that climbed from the black hole, was like that plantar's wart I painted acid on each morning to dissolve it, to dig it out of my foot; the one that, if poked exactly, made me drop to my knees: a weakness that ran like a nerve right through body to brain.

Jane and neoJane, my friend William called the phenomenon. He was still in my bed when I woke one morning, and he didn't seem to mind the little condition, and lingered. He looked like a Caravaggio or Flandrin's nude youth sitting curved and pensive against a deep evening-blue sky, a postcard of which Maggy had just sent me from Paris. William was quiet and marble and took a philosophical interest in this mind-body problem. We went to see *The Three Faces of Eve.* He left notes on strips of paper I'd cut from the emu-

and-kangaroo letterhead and placed in an envelope on my door, one of them a linguistic equation that concluded: *therefore Jane is not Jane you lose*.

To myself I wrote, *What's wrong with ignoring and forgetting things*. Like Jenny with her fairytales and songs, I made myth and literature serve. Persephone, shuttling between underworld and upper; between darkness, men, and sex, and her mother. Narcissus, frozen in his self. Echo, eaten up by need for a man who would give her nothing, until she becomes a cave. The logic of classical myth and tragedy seemed algebraic: The marble boy who refuses to love will be shattered by ruinous love. The man who refuses to know himself will be blinded by horror when at last he looks. A single crime — like feeding a man the flesh of his child, or stealing the wife of your host — can start a curse that will not be exhausted until the family, the house, is destroyed.

I didn't have a diary but on a calendar kept track, as always, of letters: *wrote to Daddy ha ha ha;* and weeks later, *letter from Daddy ha ha ha.* He wrote: *I understand why you were depressed, but one of the arts of life is to get psychologically back on top again very promptly — and to roll with the punches.*

"The problem," a psychiatrist told me at the end of a single hour when I finally made myself go to the infirmary, "is not who you are or what you do when you're blacked out. The problem is who you are when you're sober. There seems to be another person you don't allow out."

That other person never did anything too dangerous, though. Never anything like what Jenny could do. Jenny could slice her wrists and her throat. Jenny could get herself beaten up;

Jenny apparently could get herself raped. Really raped, not my little blackout affairs with Princeton men bound for Wall Street. Jenny seemed master of her abandonments. I just left myself behind.

I hope you'll understand I can't possibly respond to your "affairs"— love or non-love, my father wrote. *I can't even keep up with them. So just remain conscious of the drinking problem (ahem!) . . . Jenny is a mess and is making herself a worse one.*

So much of our growing up was defined by the negative— not being that other girl, not having that father, not having that name or country or accent. At twenty-three and twenty-two, maybe we'd both reached the hollow core, the knowledge that value was always elsewhere.

When what's inside feels like a black hole, you've got to break out and make your self *home,* somehow. Maybe it's a settler instinct: Push away from what's old and rotten, colonize a new place, make it yours. The dream: to be content, centered, not hollow. But even as I write this I know I don't mean it; such contentment may be healthy, but it's dull. One thing that split gave us, I think, was a terrible questing energy, as if the vapor inside the geode were aflame. At Princeton sometimes when I thought I'd explode and for once wouldn't let myself drink, I would escape in the old, sweet manner, by walking. Finishing a shift at Commons, I'd tear off my paper apron, stuff it in the trash, and walk hot and fast beneath the stone arch of Blair and along the slate paths that led past magnolias down through campus, then up toward the golf course. Away from all the men I'd fucked, into the woods, the Narnia fir trees, the slender green lampposts glowing to life. Then out to the open slopes and huge evening sky. Venus burned cool and quiet in the deep blue, and here were peace and excitement at once: my eyes drinking in all that fresh twilight, my mouth open to breathe it and *be* it, words in my head suddenly wanting to do more, images arising to be transformed to paper and shining graphite.

To find yourself is a phrase that's ruined but true: You go wandering, and maybe somewhere outside you do find it. But outside like this, not Jenny's way. Except for when she sat in the dark, if in Washington she still sat in the dark, with her bag and pens, and wrote poems.

After Princeton, where I finished with honors despite all the mess (*What are you going to do with your degree Jane?* wrote my father. *It is a commendable achievement,* wrote Helen. *You'll always have an admirer in me,* wrote Paul), I moved back to my mother's — a different house now, one she'd bought with her new husband, an older man, a contractor named Lou. It was the first house she'd owned, in the leafy neighborhood near Deal, and it had a screened-in porch where she'd drink coffee in her nightie among African violets, then pack up her bag with notebooks and a yogurt and walk to the Metro to go downtown to teach.

After she'd left, I'd sit on that porch in the steamy air, in the cicadas' ringing, and jab at the crossword puzzle my mother had started, stare at my horoscope that also was hers, gaze through the screen at the green haze all around, try to figure out what to do with myself. Live where? Be *what*? I made charts of possibilities that all pointed nowhere, I drew pictures of myself closed in a box. *What are you doing to do with yourself, Jane?* Teach, like my mother? Be some sort of *artist*?

I worked as an office temp for a month, typing lists for one company, making calls for another, riding around in tour buses with a tape recorder secretly reeling inside my bag for quality control of the tour guides. Finally I agreed with a friend to put everything off and spend what I'd made on a few weeks in Europe. My father, now posted there, called it a grand plan and helped pay my way.

Camping, hiking, sleeping on trains and in tiny rooms, hoarding packets of jelly and biscuits from breakfast for lunch, wandering in Geneva, Interlaken, Nice. Then my friend traveled on, leaving me in my father's new Residence, a creamy villa with a lush garden and servants and a small porcelain bell on the dining-room table when it was time to ring for coffee, a Residence where Jenny had been flown a few months before me and where I was told to act just like family. Helen sent me to galleries and pale yellow palaces or said she'd just put aside her own work again and take me herself. Then, clicking ahead of me down hallways and paths, she talked of philosophers and painters and musicians and writers, a cascade of names always splashing around her, Jugendstil, Schiele, the Secession, one name spawning three before each sentence was through, and it was astonishing that after Princeton I still knew so little, sputtering out a few lines about ruins or myth as I floated behind like a fish, gaping.

It was the ionic wind, of course, she said. The *Föhne*. It exhausted everyone.

Then back to Washington to try living again, to figure out what to *do* with myself. *I'm sorry to hear that you had such a difficult month arguing with yourself over D.C. or N.Y.,* Helen wrote. *We missed you when you left, and still.*

Helen has written ever since New York, pages covered in cursive, with photos or gallery postcards tucked in the folds, images she knows I'd like to see or would like to remember. *Aren't these photos marvelous? The series of you by candlelight is broken because we put the third one in a frame.* Rolling blue words about my troubles or plans (*We understand that you want to get on with your life . . . and become self-sufficient as soon as possible too*); and about books, painters, films, ideas (*I named one large painting "Echo," remembering the paper you sent us last year*). And always—until a point—a few lines about Jenny. *I will be trying to see what, if anything, we can work out for Jenny's future. I don't know when I'll be in the States again; so it's crucial.*

When I read Helen's letters, I don't find the doubled surface I've seen when we're together—the twinned surface born of our twinned families—as when you move a piece of moiré silk in the light and the hues change, sweet pink suddenly shot through with blood-black. Maybe in letters, written alone before a fire, more tender feelings can come out; or maybe letters form a record and must be written with care. But when Helen and I have been together, in one moment she could be the woman who wrote those letters, could be with someone she truly liked, a gentle blue light spilling over me as we forgot who we were, spoke loosely, laughed, and I could almost feel the fierce mother she surely was for her girls — but in the next moment I would say something wrong and seem to remind her who I was: not Jenny, a girl Jenny was not, a girl who'd gotten everything.

Helen's made it as if I've won out as far as fathers go, leaving Jenny with none.

A gate would shut, and eyes that had just sparkled with humor would turn glassy against me. We'd stand apart, words silent between us — or there might be a cool, pink smile and a glimpse through the mirror: *We have often wondered where you came from. You look nothing at all like Edward.*

So many mirrors in this family, so hard to know where to set your foot or tentatively place your hand.

Back in Washington, I did at last get a job and an apartment, and William moved down from Philly. I don't know whether someone said Jenny was missing and asked me to look for her, or whether I just wanted to or thought I should, but I did. *Thanks for trying to find Jenny,* my father wrote. *It would mean a lot, especially to Helen, if you could try again.*

I found her tending bar on Eighteenth Street, at Café Lautrec. On the façade was an enormous Lautrec mural of a man in a black hat and crimson scarf, and inside was a faux French café: pressed-tin ceiling, tiled floor, a long bar on which people tap danced, a mirror behind it reflecting rows of glasses and colored bottles and faces, and standing before them, Jenny.

"My *god,*" she cried when I came in from the sun, "it's my

sister!" She strutted around the bar with her cocky Jenny walk and flung her silver-bangled arms around me. She was slim again, pretty and haughty Fifth Avenue Jenny, all that mirror behind her as she strode back and forth among the glasses and bottles and knew the names of the men who came in, and knew just what they wanted. She was bright and wired, and talked rapid-fire about a job or two or maybe three she'd had before this one but lost because of some scandal or absurd accusation, something to do with her and the owner and the owner's wife, but it was all just *piss,* she said, and laughed, and then got her proud Corinthia look and gazed into the air at the other self no one acknowledged and with whom she privately communed. Then she snapped back to life and turned electric again, her eyes dangerously bright and her fingers digging into my skin, looking like nothing could hold her inside her own.

I went to Café Lautrec a lot. William, too; he worked as a paralegal downtown and had stopped in there once and seen Jenny without knowing she was my famous stepsister. It was fun to sit on barstools and watch her; she'd give us drinks or just toss the bill. I'd be beat at closing, but not William and Jenny, and they'd go to after-hours clubs. Nothing special, he'd report when he came home: girls in dark corners making out, lots of coke.

At first, Jenny was slim in a white T-shirt and black pants. Then she started to swell, the pants straining until she'd leave the shirt untucked or wear one of her big men's shirts, and then again she'd shrink, turn to wire. She drank prodigiously, did lots of coke, became fascinated with caves and depths and learned spelunking and diving, and still evidently went at herself with knives.

After a year I lost her again, and my father and Helen wrote of salvage operations. Paul shook his head and said that he wished to hell they'd leave Jenny alone and quit feeding her plane tickets to Europe; the only way she'd ever be able to pull herself together was on her own. But in 1985 she was flown back to Canberra, where my father was posted again. Her plans weren't clear. She'd need a visa to stay in Australia, so apparently she was still American. If she figured herself out she might move to Sydney.

My plans weren't any clearer than hers. *What are you going to do with yourself, Jane?* Some people look around clearly from the start: heads in the air, eyes open, all the world airy, a chance. They have an idea, an urgency that governs the days, while others lurch in rain forests and mud looking for some lost thing they need back in place before they can even begin.

Idling. A few months after Jenny left, I decided to go to Australia, too. No plans, just that antipodal pull; it suddenly was the place to go.

Sometimes it was the continent itself that pulled: that coral-colored island swimming in a blue sea, the whiff of an ancient, innocent, lost land, the screams of birds over crashing waves. That fabulist place of bottlebrushes, banksias, gum leaves, koalas, the paired emu and kangaroo: I pictured that continent somehow taking me *in*. But then the fantasy altered, and instead it was a man on a motorcycle or in a car who roared out of the red earth and just *took* me.

Making men your home. Such a faulty quest, a hopeless roundabout route. Like Odysseus and all his women in their seaside lairs, ten years wandering toward home.

My father approved of the trip and helped pay my way: *It will always be in your blood and consciousness, is a very special place, and so you must at least get a mature impression of it . . . Do you have dates? Cost? A booking? Get your act together.*

Paul thought it interesting, too, although those brows rose skeptical at the idea that there could be anything to *see* in an ass-backward place like Australia. He gave me a bag of Nixon pens and black State Department penknives and a blue notebook commemorating Reagan's trip to Korea.

"It's good to travel with things like this, you know, Jane," he said, and grinned, and paused for the punch line. "So you've got something shiny to fob off on the natives."

The Qantas flew over the Pacific in darkness for a day and a half, the stars shifting, Venus moving in her transit, Venus who had first lured Banks and Captain Cook. The night went on and on and would not open up into day, as if, were you fast enough, you could fly in perpetual darkness. But just as the sun slipped free of the rim, that last continent appeared like a miracle in the wrinkled ocean, and sunlight struck its edge, making it glow crimson against the blue water and white breaks of waves.

Flight attendants walked down the aisles spraying disinfectant so we wouldn't dirty the ancient new island, and I was almost sick with excitement. I went through immigration, hoping my birthplace would be noted, it wasn't, I waited for luggage, passed into the arrivals hall. Then a door slid open to Australia. It seems now that it was a huge door, a hangar door, a whole wall that simply slid open, and there in the blinding morning sun stood a dark form, there in the light stood Jenny.

Surely I'd been told he couldn't meet me, yet I'd expected him, somehow. But of course I hadn't expected him, I didn't need to think this but knew it hard as I walked toward her in the sun; why would I ever expect him? This journey had nothing to do with him. It was nothing like Jenny's disastrous journey the other way across the Pacific. I was just coming to see my home, or find a man with a motorcycle or car, any man anywhere who would take me.

Helen and Jenny and I stayed in a hotel in King's Cross, and Jenny seemed electric, wanting to fly into Sydney after months trapped in Canberra. We sped in a hydrofoil over the blue bays Cook had first seen two centuries earlier, over the water into which the *Oronsay* had steamed. We went to Port Manly and Bondi, a seaside town with a famous beach that was quiet that day, empty in Australia's spring. The day was windy and bright, our hair snapping at our cheeks, faces fresh with salt air.

"I love this bit here, *come* on," Jenny said, and pulled me from the road up the grassy hillside. We walked up a sandy trail lined with blowing grass, along the high, windy rim of the cliff, the jagged edge of the continent standing in blue water. Up there we stopped and forgot who we were, just looked out at the enormous shining Pacific, spread our arms, shut our eyes, took mouthfuls of wind, and both loved, as always, the same things.

Later, bars. Helen urged me not to give Jenny money, not to buy her drinks, but I wouldn't listen, liked having money that came from a good job despite *What* are *you going to* do *with yourself, Jane?* We broke out into dark, granite Sydney, Jenny yanking me in her terrible sharp shoes, and climbed up ballroom stairs and through a black velvet curtain into a hall of thunder and spinning disco balls. I bought her drinks and we shouted over the music, and her eyes flashed in all directions as she looked for someone or something until suddenly she found it. She whispered hot and fast in my ear before going, but I couldn't hear what. So I found my way back to the hotel, to Helen, and didn't need to tell her what had happened.

To South Australia, then, to the traces of the more ancient family, the lines that had sailed from Britain and Ireland to plant themselves and make this new world. Dora, Maisie, and Albert; aunts, uncles, new cousins. They took me to the spot where Colonel Light landed; to Victor Harbour, where my father was born; to the brick Anglican church where my parents married. They showed me the first pictures I ever saw of the two, my mother in her white angled satin, my father looking nervous with his thin neck. They showed me live kangaroos and emus and put a heavy koala in my arms, just as they'd pressed a stuffed one into Maggy's and my arms twenty years earlier, so we'd never forget where we came from.

After two weeks I let the lost accent settle on my tongue, began talking with a faux-Aussie lilt.

Then at last to Canberra, and my father. I believe he thought it important that the city and country be properly shown, but whether he represented them, or they him, I don't know. He drove me to ancient sites, a silent tour of secret history: Lake Burley Griffin, where he'd knelt like a suitor between Maggy and me; Rocky Knob, where the magpies screamed; the little house we'd lived in — irksome places, saturated with the internalized past, with the private acts of those parents. I don't remember talking about the meaning of these places, or talking much about anything. A cloud had seeped into my head, sunk from the marble sky.

Memory seems such a funny substance, built of the physical world around you but then transformed into private ephemera. To see still living, dimensional, and *real* the places that formed that private tissue is disorienting. Here was actually the house where my mother vamped in her yellow swimsuit for Paul; here was the driveway where she sobbed as she hurried Maggy and me in our nighties into the old blue car; here was the rock at the bottom of the street where I'd sit and wait for my father to come home. And here, above all, was that man himself, who in one body contained the mythic lost figment into whose arms I'd dreamt of flying all those nights, and the real man near whom I was so rigid and angry I could not say a word. We walked through dry grass among gum trees, and I was waxen because the long, thin leaves and peeling bark, the silky red bottlebrush, the barnacled banksias, the personal arboretum that had lived in my ribs, was now outside and figured by him, and I could no longer love it.

He walked with me up Rocky Knob, always a little ahead or behind. He jingled the keys in his pocket and smiled here and there, not quite catching my eye. He took pictures of me before that house, that gum tree, those dinosaur stones, documenting the moment of return, like glossy proofs that there were no hard feelings, everything had turned out just fine.

In these photos I look grim and embarrassed. I'm wondering what to do, what to say, feeling that miserable matted past all around and unable to utter a word. Perhaps he's feeling the same. Perhaps he's wishing to god he didn't have this problem, this bitter rigid daughter, when there are nuclear tests, relations with China, so many real issues to deal with.

My father and I had one easy thing in common, smoking, and because Helen believed he'd quit he had to smoke secretly, so this formed a rebellious camaraderie. When the sickening silence became overwhelming, one of us would pull out a cigarette and there'd be a burst of relief: wrappers, matches, something to do with the hands, a few stock phrases about this bad habit to utter, the peaceful exhaling.

We drove out of Canberra along roads he'd probably driven in 1965, racing that other car to one of those eucalypt picnics. In the countryside we watched a mob of kangaroos leap up a green hillside, and my father seemed pleased that Australia performed as it ought. He took me to a preserve of tall, thin gums and said, "Now you've got to find a koala. To prove you're really Australian. Can't be Australian without spotting a koala! Off you go. Give it a try."

It was protocol, a silly thing he'd surely invented to absorb that wretched energy, but I spent the afternoon with my head cocked back, staring as if my life depended on it, sick and angry, staring up into those tall, skinny gum trees, trying to find a miserable clump of gray fur huddled in a fork in the branches, and finally, after two hours, I did. So that was a subject, it warranted a photo, documentation that I was truly Australian, and as he readied the camera I raged in silence about needing to prove this and decided maybe I didn't *want* to prove this, maybe I wanted to throw ass-backward Australia away, and how was it I'd lost my claim to it, anyway, and why was it that no proof, none, had ever been worth a thing; and after the business of taking this photo was through we hurried back to the cigarettes.

So it went, the weird barometric pressure of Canberra compounding the weird barometric pressure inside: so much inside that would never be said; so much outside pushing in, reminding.

Maybe it was the same for both of us, because one night, after we'd visited a painter friend and had been drinking wine all afternoon, back at home, in the kitchen, my father kept drinking and suddenly transformed. As if a light had been switched off, or on. All at once blackness streamed out.

His face changed as he looked at me across the table, and there was a weird gap in the air, a coiling. Then out of nowhere, in a different voice, he began to speak of "drunkenness and cruelty." Had I ever heard that? Did I know those were the terms of divorce, the trumped-up terms put on paper by my mother? And did I know it was a bloody lie?

I stared at those pale eyes that didn't seem to see me but things he'd nursed for twenty years.

Did I know how much that charge had cost him? And how my grandmother Dora had watched my mother have an affair on the ship but never said a word? Did I know about this? Had my mother ever told me?

What she did on the ship, he said. What she did on that bloody ship. His eyes fixed me like pins, but seemed to see her. At twenty-three in a Canberra kitchen I *was* her, full of the things she'd done that had cost him and of the stories he seemed to think she'd told against him ever since.

I ran to my room, which of course wasn't mine but Jenny's, and stood there as if something would actually crack in my ribs, but couldn't move, couldn't leave, I didn't have enough money and this was the place I'd wanted to come, the place that had pulled for twenty years, so all I could do was smoke, hard, and stare up at the Southern Cross.

The following morning: no trace in his eyes. Or maybe they were the eyes I'd had so often at Princeton, shocked by that other dark self, afraid of what might have slipped out: I don't know. He peered at me over coffee and asked what I'd planned for the day. Perhaps I ought to have a look at Canberra's new Parliament House. Hmm? Very worth seeing, a most interesting structure, much of it underground, just a bus ride away.

————

Why should I care and feel any sort of personal involvement? I wrote small and neat in Paul's blue Reagan notebook as I lay with the door locked, on Jenny's bed.

> *It strikes deep, deeper than it should. I wasn't the one left. I was just one of the ones left . . . They have all finished with it and we are only beginning . . . The lack of shame disturbs me. The lack of questions does, too. Don't they want to know what wreckage there may have been? I like Jenny because she shows it most . . . Once again, how much does it matter.*

Jenny was staying somewhere else while I visited; she'd had to leave, of course, to make room for me. I was told this lightly as I sat on her bed. I had displaced her again, I was always displacing her, leaving her fatherless, homeless. She now raged around Canberra, which once had been mine but now was hers, because surely she had displaced me, too, and after the night of drunkenness and cruelty the only thing to do was bolt out and rage with her. We walked fast across stretches of grass between empty suburban roads, Jenny in her ridiculous shoes, her hair too glamorous, coiffed for elsewhere. We smoked as we'd smoked when she'd come to my Washington to claim my stepfather, exhaling hard into the sky. We sat on curbs or at the feet of statues in this antipodean Anglo capital city. We got up and walked fast anywhere else, and talked as we walked, but whatever we said fell into the air and I don't know if it ever came close to the subject; how could we even find the right pronouns.

We went to bars, smoked more, drank cocktails, screamed over music, and staggered home late enough to be noticed: twenty years after we sat in our bathtub, two aging, maddened girls pressed foot to foot. I'd developed a roll of film, some shot in D.C., with the Olympus Paul had given me for graduation, and at a screeching bar one night I showed Jenny pictures: black-and-white William at the beach on the sand like a pensive Flandrin, William I'd written to four times already and who had written back only once; Tommy, Jenny's boy and mine, jumping delirious in my mother's backyard. Jenny looked at both pictures sweetly, head tilted, with her private smile.

And then glancing at one photo she said, "There's your apartment," before clapping her hand to her mouth. A picture of the wooden Murphy table and benches that folded out of the wall like an insect, the table where I'd been drawing Daedalus's tiny moves toward the air. I looked at her in the dark, blaring bar; she looked back laughing through her fingers, through that old mirror, that moat between beds. Because she'd never been to my apartment with me. When I was away once, it seemed she'd gone there with William.

"Oh *come* on, Jane," she said, grabbing my arm. "I made a point of remembering he was with *you*! So of course I didn't let him —" and she broke off, laughing, so all I could do was shrug, light a cigarette, order a drink, and look around for anyone who would do, any damned man at the party to take. I found him fast. And fucked him that night in his car, after we dropped Jenny off at the house of my father's superior, where she climbed in the window of my father's superior's young son.

It was October, nearly our birthday, and Helen kept saying, "We must have a party. My god, how often have you been together on your birthday?" On the day, Jenny was in the house only a moment before she left again, apparently thrown out. Maybe she told Helen whose window she'd climbed in, or maybe her eyes were not looking right: I don't know. Voices rose, and I opened the door just as Jenny strode past, staring ahead with that Corinthia smile, looking pleased at having been thrown out again, as if she wouldn't know herself otherwise. She didn't look at me or say good-bye, her heels leaving a trail of pocks in the floor.

When I headed back to Sydney, Helen warned me that Jenny would call and want money, and she urged me again not to give it. I didn't know what Jenny wanted money for and wouldn't ask. In Sydney I dragged my bags from the station to a hotel in King's Cross, maybe the same hotel I was told the four adults had stayed in twenty years earlier. My father was to join me the next day, but meanwhile I had the man I'd met in the bar, who lived in Sydney and followed me up. Every night I'd have dinner with my father at Italian restaurants, and now that he'd erupted once, we both drank hard and gave it free rein—at least at night; our slow fights over garlic prawns and wine always vanished by morning.

I'd slowly revolve my glass of red wine and say again and again, "But you're not listening. What I'm telling you is that not only do I not love you, but I don't even like you. I don't care about you at all."

And he'd laugh through his trim beard and tell me that of course I loved him, I just didn't know it, I had to love him because he was my father, I had no choice in the matter. Which only made me drink more wildly and go blacker. Then he'd return to the hotel, and I'd go meet my man with the car. We'd go to clubs, dance, do coke and fuck in bathroom stalls, then fuck again in the hotel, with Daddy two rooms down, all this fucking that was still utterly numb, I couldn't feel anything, just had a man in my bed as proof. I'd sleep an hour and then get up sick to see the sights of Sydney with my father, until finally it was time to leave.

When we said good-bye what always happened at that moment happened once more. He hugged me and smiled with blinking wet eyes, suddenly seeming to see me for the first time, and as I walked down the gangplank to leave him and Australia, I felt that tug in my stomach and couldn't believe I'd ruined it, I hadn't even known what I'd come for but was losing it again.

Flying over the Pacific for a day and a half, to or away from home. *I'm just telling you one thing. Don't ever leave yourself behind.* It's hard to keep track of time in the air, only gassy deep sky above and glinting sea below, and somewhere the invisible date line and time zones. Sick from drinking and coke, I focused on not throwing up or crying and kept trying to fix what time it was in that tube of air, kept trying to fix anything in all that dissolved. A pull in my stomach, that gravitational pull, as if all those loose tubes would just slither out.

Somewhere down there was the equator. Once, on ships like Cook's and Humboldt's, there had been a ceremony upon crossing it, as the known world turned upside down, and maybe it's when we'd crossed the line ourselves that Maggy and I took that cocoa bath and put on grassy hula skirts. That line lay somewhere, and if I could only calculate the time zones and fix where I was in the sky, I'd know when we flew over it, and this seemed so important, knowing exactly when I went back to the other side.

The Qantas's shadow flew far below on the water's surface, and watching it I imagined I was down there, too, inside the little shape flitting over the waves, a shadow no longer bound to my foot but free. Maybe this is the original act of imagination: to marvel when you see an image cast on the wall of a cave by light, then to make an image with the shadows of your hands or with pigment, an image animated by your absent yet projected self. In one stroke, you extend yourself but also slip out, out of that skin, that jar, that impossible house, and instead make something that's worthy.

9

A man on a motorcycle, a man in a car. Speed has something to do with it, being borne away anywhere else. Being held in that space has something to do with it, too. But most of all it's the man. *Just take me.* I want to close my eyes and not be here, I want to disappear and dissolve into you, I do not want to be my self. Just take me wherever you're going.

After William, because there always had to be someone, came Anthony. He'd been an architecture grad student at Princeton and was thirty-seven to my twenty-four, tall and lined, with dark silvering hair and an arrogant walk, part Irish, part Lebanese, all Baltimore, elegant and artsy in a beat leather jacket and motorcycle boots, scarred from a crash and a knifing, full of stories of his rock-and-roll past and bad-boy behavior, all the beauties who'd come before me, and the intricate ways he'd betrayed them. As of Princeton, he'd been remaking himself.

He had a prize to study Islamic architecture and on a first date drove me up Massachusetts Avenue to the mosque. In blue espadrilles and orange pants, he parked wherever he wanted, no rules, and strode around pointing out details of screens, pools, geometric decor. He drove me through Rock Creek Park, he drove me to Rehoboth, he drove me to Baltimore, Boston, New York. I was the golden girl, he said; he'd been watching and hoping forever. His hands always trembled, the lines he drew trembled. The idea of his face drawing near mine was too much, but drinking always helped; I disappeared until it was over. Then eight years after the night on the lounge chair with Sutter, on a pair of twin beds that kept sliding apart in an apartment on East Eighty-third, I finally broke open and acquired knowledge of that famous thing the girls had taunted me about so often a few blocks north.

I wore Anthony's shirts, drank his espresso, slept in his bed, spoke his words—*fascist, hip, aesthete.* I stopped shaving my underarms because he liked it, let my hair go wild because he liked it, wore little tight leopard-print dresses. I walked out of my own place and moved into him whole. I'd applied to graduate school because I didn't know what else to do, and when I packed my books and clothes and dishes and moved to Providence, Anthony got a job in Boston and came, too.

But the *Iliad* seemed so remote, with its ancient betrayal and exhausting battles: so many words for *shinguard* to look up and forget. It was much easier to climb into Anthony, lie in there dreamy, and turn off the light. Golden girl: I lay like an odalisque on a futon on the dirty floor, and he would look at me with eyes so hungry that without moving I drew him to me, pulled him on a current I felt silky in my hand. No need for anyone else, not friends or a mother; no need for any other man to see me, and dangerous if one did. I lived among his Persian rugs and Bauhaus stools and neogothic prints. He was more in love than he'd ever been, he said; he'd never loved anyone like this, he said; it just kept getting better.

I abandoned classics and moved on with Anthony, to Boston, Washington, Miami, following his jobs teaching architecture or designing. Like foreign posts, always starting new. My grandfather Albert started his letters *Dear Meandering Jane*. My father wrote, *Come out of hibernation. Remember me? If nothing else I come through once a year around your birthday.* I saved whatever letters found their way through the change-of-address stamps and didn't fly out of all the beat boxes and vans. But my father seemed as remote as the *Iliad*, a painful, numb thing locked back in the chest, except for once a year, when I saw him. Yet when my grandmother Maisie died, right after my father had left Australia on one of his trips to the United States, and he had to fly straight back upon landing, my awful first crestfallen thought was: Now I won't see him this year.

Jenny occasionally called Albert for money, but I didn't learn why she needed it until later. She was living in Sydney, sometimes *the most together in history,* otherwise smashing herself again. I heard little of what she was up to. She had a monstrous boyfriend who would not sit in chairs and couldn't in my father's house, anyway, because evidently he was not allowed in, being, among other things I didn't know at the time, a New Zealander living on the Australian dole. What Jenny needed money for: I could have known if I'd listened. Helen cared continually and tried hard, wrote my father, but you would need to be a saint.

I still didn't know what to do with myself. *What are you going to do, Jane?* What to do, what to be. I found work whenever Anthony and I moved, jobs as a production artist or editor. What I kept was drawing, getting lost in that fabulous current between whatever I looked at and my eyes, my hand. With colored pencils I drew emus and parrots at the National Zoo; in Miami, I sat on the tough grass of South Beach and drew tropical fronds and modernist curves. I rewrote and illustrated the story of Amor and Psyche, a girl listening for a rustle at the window, obsessed with unclaimable Love; I put Psyche in a Miami world of coral rock and sea.

Beauty exists in the air between the object and your eyes and makes you want to dissolve, be what you see, *have* the beauty you see, although there is no having other than looking. Ancient ideas of beauty and love: Both enter through the eyes and undo you. I drew Anthony, his sleeping, oblivious foot resting on an elegant graphite calf. I could draw anywhere; so why not follow Anthony? So much easier to climb in that car, close my eyes, and open my mouth to the rushing breeze.

That a father would be home is built into the language. But any man can be home, be the source of a pull as strong as the pull toward home, when you are away from him.

You drew yourself to be Psyche, wrote Paul. *Are you? In your myth, Psyche has no influence over her own destiny. Do you feel that way?*

———

After we'd been in Miami two months, when I'd just started work as an editor, Anthony was asked to teach a term in Venice. Follow him again? What to do, what to be! My father and Helen were living in Italy. *You are __mad__ not to come with Anthony,* Helen wrote. *Italy is the perfect place to develop and expand tastes . . . You simply mustn't allow yourself such __pedestrian__ thoughts as that you are somehow losing 5 months.*

When I see myself now following Anthony to Venice, where I'd go out every day with my sketchbook and pencils, I see myself stepping into Helen, stepping along a line she had drawn. Trailing after her over the years, staying near: as she moved through a gallery and with magic persuaded a guard to unlock a secret room so she could stand before a Grünewald, before its gorgeous, hideous colors, and have me stand beside her, and together, whispering, we explored its layers, and I managed to notice something unusual, and she turned to me with wondering blue eyes and said, But I've never seen that! Yet it's perfectly true. Edward, come here. Darling: Jane's just said something so interesting.

Trailing after Helen, staying near: as she moved through markets, past stands heaped with ice and tentacles and gleaming blue fish, or through wooden stalls bearing quilted greens and saffron flowers. Then watching in the kitchen as she performed the magic of frying a flower gold, although in my own kitchen later I produced a floppy mess. Following her through narrow streets to places where you could buy not only the best shoes, not only such ordinary objects of desire, but specially made parchment and pigments: She led me to a small shop like a *Wunderkammer,* a smell of mineral intensity when we stepped through the door, wooden tables with boxes of waxy or powdered pigments that filled my nostrils with the urge to *make*. She chose what she wanted, and we left with packets of substanced color with which she would create paintings that were inscrutable, although I tried hard to read them, although I understood the ideas of the Golden Mean and illegible languages, still they were inscrutable, and she shrugged my puzzling away and gave me instead a painting I could read, as she has given me banksia cones whose tiny barnacle mouths she has painted coral, as she has given me etchings of the Tomb of the Baker and of Lady Godiva ringed by nude men in trees, because she knows my tastes and fascinations. She knows because she's helped me create them.

So, leaving my editing job, paycheck, daily bus ride to work, flying after Anthony to Venice, I stepped into Helen. I'd shop in the fish market at the Rialto, walk to a different church each day, stand in the frigid air, ice breathing into my boots, and draw *grotteschi*, caryatids, marble mergirls, copy the rose and gold damasks of Bellini's saints. Or I'd find a shop that Helen had told me sold the drawing board I needed, with a certain crisp finish, perfect for grinding in bright color. And as I did these things I'd see her figure lightly moving before me. A pattern of life Helen had shown, not my mother; this life had nothing to do with my mother, and as I stepped into it I both wanted it and felt sick, as always, at the betrayal.

Although also this — with another shift of the moiré silk, another lovely della Francesca smile: I understood, didn't I, that the drawings I did were just illustration? Of course they weren't properly *art*.

After Venice, Anthony and I moved to New Orleans, where we both worked at Tulane; he taught, I wrote proposals and speeches. But the following semester, he won a fellowship for a year in Italy, across the river from my father and Helen, and once more I would quit my job and go, too. Jenny would also be there a few months: Another rescue operation, my father said. So, five years after our birthday nonparty in Canberra, Jenny and I were to see each other again.

Anthony flew to Europe ahead of me to get settled while I finished a project, found someone to take our apartment and care for the cat, and applied for a visa as his "wife."

Whenever he left, it was terrible exposure: insulation gone, skin stripped bare and too soft in the scalding world. Our apartment was the second floor of an old yellow house on the edge of the Garden District, lopsided, leaky, a listing ship, rattling and shaking whenever trucks barreled past. The windows had no screens, so anoles darted in and ran up the walls, and palmetto bugs tumbled in at night. One planted her eggs in the silverware drawer, which I learned when they hatched one night and the forks began clinking. There was a gunshot hole in the living-room ceiling, and when it rained, which it did every day after Anthony left, water sputtered in.

I got my visa and packed and gave notice at work. But just as I was about to leave, Anthony called to say maybe I didn't want to come, maybe I should wait.

"I don't know," he said. "You might not be happy here. It's cold. I don't think you'll like it."

Yes, my father said when I called, he and Helen thought they'd seen Anthony going about town with a woman. A very attractive woman, in fact. An artist, as it turned out.

The same question, the impossible question: What makes one woman, one packet of flesh and the being inside it, so drenched in value as to make a man leave a woman he loved, leave even his own daughters? I don't understand what love is, how its object is contained in a single skin, how that object exerts irresistible pull. Or: I understand it when I feel the closest thing to love I feel. It's this: That other person has become home, and to be apart from him is to be in exile, helplessly gravitating toward wherever he is, having no center of your own.

And another question, one I keep asking myself, and as I grow older the problem only grows worse: Why is jealousy obliterating? Why is the vision of another woman taking your place ruinous? You don't die. You're still there. Your forearms are there with the light hair on them, your stomach sucked in at the jeans, your bruised knees. You haven't been obliterated. Yet it feels as if you have. You've just made the mistake, again, of granting your existence to someone else's eyes.

Between writing speeches, I stood in bathroom stalls at Tulane and cried, tears actually dropping at my feet. At home, rain streamed around the windows and doors; it dripped through the cracks and gunshot hole in the ceiling, and when the grass outside turned to water, the place seemed to keel. The windows didn't lock or even close right, anyone could slide them open from outside, and at midnight I'd go from window to window to make sure no one was climbing up the sides of the house. I'd stick my head out and crane around in the dark, then close the window as hard as I could. The apartment had sixteen windows plus a porch door out back, and by the time I'd checked them all and returned to the first window, I'd realize that something might have happened since the last round, someone might have slunk down Louisiana Avenue and ducked into my dark yard and might be out there right now, peering up, so I'd do the whole thing over. Finally, at 2:00 in the morning, I'd have to give up, so I'd lie down on the futon on the floor and pull the sheets up to my neck, run my eyes without blinking from one corner of the ceiling to the other and down to the floor and then from one corner of the floor to the other and then back up to the ceiling until everything was as sealed as it could be. Then, still without blinking, I'd turn off the light. But within a minute I'd turn it on again, to make sure nothing was crawling toward me. Not a palmetto bug, or an anole, or even a murderer, nothing simple like these, but a hand. I was a grown person who wrote speeches for the president of Tulane, but at night I switched the light on and off and on and off and on and off, sobbing, afraid a severed hand was crawling toward me in the dark.

When I finally made myself go to a therapist, it took her just an hour to see that perhaps this new split was reopening the others, opening up all sorts of old mess. The blackout sex, the crawling hands, the bedtime rituals, the disappearing, the dissolution because of Anthony — clearly it all wound back to the split, to the situation with the fathers. And I'd just had a bad Pap smear, and everything felt like utter black ruin. But this therapist was kind and found the family story so much more compelling than her usual fare that she charged me only half price. Which helped save money for my trip.

Because I did go, just not for the magical year with my "husband" near my father. I went on a desperate mission to win Anthony back from the attractive artist, from a safe base in my father's Residence, and to take care of Albert when he visited and my father and Helen had to travel, as I'd promised.

I'd miss Jenny again, but Anthony didn't. Just before he told me that maybe I didn't want to come, my father and Helen had him up to the Residence for dinner, while Jenny was still there. She had a whole evening to watch him and listen to his jokes and stories and see him look satisfied and run a hand through his hair, and afterward she said only one thing: "It's amazing. He's exactly like Father."

Helen told me this after I'd landed, as I sat bleary at the dining-room table, bright paintings and mirrors all around. I'd come with gaudy earrings, lipsticks, a frolicky dress for my mission, and when Helen told me what Jenny had said, it was like a pane of clouded glass rubbed clear in my head: Anthony *was* like Paul. Of course he was. He *was* Paul. Which made what I was doing there even more sickly, more entrenched in the fathers, and I split open before her right there on the table, spilled out how Anthony and Paul slurred together inside me, men and fathers and crawling hands and blackness, that split running right through my core.

Helen and my father left the next day. So the Residence was empty, just Albert, me, the chef, the Nigerian staff. Albert gamely marched with me down Parioli to the Ara Pacis and ancient squares. He whistled and recited lines of Romantic poetry about ruins as he peered from beneath a hand withered by the antipodean sun at this antique new world. When he'd been tucked into bed at nine and lay like a pontifical statue, I had nothing to do in that Residence but roam.

From outside you had to buzz at the gate to be let in, then cross cobblestones through rosebushes toward the brick and fossil-white, stripped-classical palace. Wide, bright terraces jutted out, and a cold pool lay deep in the garden. There was a porch for harangues and a living room so cavernous it had three archipelagos of sofas and took a long time to walk through. Above this formal floor rose three or four more, reached by a wide, carpeted staircase, an elevator, and invisible stairs for the staff. The place was crowned by a tower, where you could stand on a marble floor so brilliant in the sun it hurt your head and look down at the Stadio Olimpico, the snaking brown river, umbrella pines on the hills in the haze. You couldn't get out, though; because before Samuel and Ahmed disappeared for the night, they rolled the security gates over the windows.

A formal house, a Residence, turned out for function — the public rooms downstairs, of course, but even those on the family floors, because this family must always represent. I roamed up the wide staircase past the bright paintings that had traveled from New York to Canberra to here; I wandered soundless down the wide, pale hall, no bamboo here, just padding, hunting feet. I wandered into my father and Helen's room. Plumped pillows, silken tassels, mirrors, composed as a painting. I looked at the big framed pictures of the girls. I looked in the closets, at the sheathed clothes and rows of polished shoes. I looked at the jewelry box, the neat leather clothes brush and mirror and combs, the room and its objects bespeaking marriage as art, accoutered, in well-crafted collusion.

Sixty silent paces back up the hall to the room where Jenny had stayed. It was on the family floor, not the formal gold-and-green guest suite in which I'd been installed, with instructions on tipping the staff. But there was no trace of her here, none of the treasures that were also mine, none of the names that were also mine, carved into the desk or lipsticked on the mirror. No pet skull or trash or bloodstains on the carpet, not even any ruinous shoes.

I've seen pictures of Jenny there, taken just before I arrived, in that big Parioli villa, photos taken in spots where photos were later taken of me, as if we could never occupy a space without displacing each other. She stands in the garden before a wall of ivy, laughing at a marble *grottescho* that leers from the green. Her hands are clenched, her eyes squeezed shut, the smile the only thing that shows pleasure. She wears culottes, as she'd worn in New York almost twenty years earlier. Her knees are bare and look scuffed and awkward: a little girl's knees, but old. She'd been there a few months, worked at some job. She'd been trying to sort herself out and managed, mostly, but one night evidently she got out—how, I don't know, but here's what I picture: I see her roaming through those pale carpeted halls like a maddened thirty-year-old Goldilocks until finally she just smashes out of those gates, goes running down Parioli.

She ended up in a man's car, and what happened then I don't know, but I think she was dumped somewhere alone. I keep seeing this: Jenny waking up in a field outside the city, a field of scarlet poppies like in *The Wizard of Oz* but unframed, unfriendly. I see her looking down at her scuffed dirty knees, feeling the scratches on her back, touching a finger between her legs for the usual information, and wondering which way was home.

From Jenny's nonroom I drifted down the soundless staircase, oversized to make you small. Into my father's study: spears and boomerangs on the walls; his desk, scrolled and polished; his emu-and-kangaroo stationery; his gold Cross pens, where all those blue words had been born.

In the vast living room, on coffee tables and shelves, was his collection of small silver boxes. He'd bought them in Asia, Africa, the Middle East, beautiful silver boxes in animal or geometric forms or rustic and lumpen, with tiny silver clasps. They gleamed, so small, so appealing, anything might be inside, there must be something; for millennia, girls have been hoping.

I started at the top left corner of one shelf and picked up the first little silver box and opened it. Not even dust, the inside wiped clean. I shut the latch and replaced the box on the shelf, picked up the next one. Empty. I closed it and put it back on the shelf. The small silver turtle, the elephant, the cube. I picked up each and looked in each and closed each and returned it to its spot, and each time I held a cool little heart — this time there'd be something.

They were all empty, I'd already known that. But if there had been another room with a hundred more silver boxes, if the entire Residence had been a mausoleum of silver boxes, I would have opened each, poked my finger inside, shaken it, to find what must someday be there.

Before my father collected silver boxes, he'd collected antique blue soda bottles. At another time, he'd collected pewter. Also Audubon prints. People collect to fill the space around them? All that empty time? To fill themselves, like ballast, give themselves weight against a terrible pull that tells them the center is elsewhere? Is the center always elsewhere?

I would say that I collect nothing, I like throwing things out, except I've saved almost every letter my father and Paul and any other man have written me, love letters starting from when I was seven, notes left on my door, postcards sent by men I don't even remember.

Dolce Vita. I went out in my lipstick, sundress, and high heels, down Parioli, past couples clasping in the grass, to the Pincio for trysts with Anthony. But this won me only a dinner and walk and an aborted fuck behind some shrubs in a park.

He looked at me but didn't see me, had invested all his gold elsewhere.

The night my father and Helen returned, at dinner with Albert in the dining room overlooking Jenny's ivied garden, my father turned to me and whispered, "How about meeting in an hour or so, after Dad's in bed, up in the tower to have a bottle of bomb?"

I glided through the salon and up the carpeted staircase, into the dream of the airplane, the tarmac, the glorious union. In the gold-tasseled suite, I washed my face and put on that same lipstick and sundress. Then paced, looking out the window across the gleaming river, toward the Villa Farnesina and the lowering sun. Then up in clattering heels to the tower.

But again I'd somehow forgotten about Helen. Because of course she was there, what had I thought, a date alone with my father? I sat on a plump floral sofa, heels hard and shaky on the marble floor, with the city melting all around, while my father fussed with the prosecco cork. He poured, said, Cheers, chaps! and we three clinked and sipped.

Then Helen leaned back into her flowers and said, Jane. Don't you think it's time we talked about all this? About the problem you've always had with me — as the other woman?

Vespas wailed down the Via Flaminia, the sun sank glaring into the haze, and my father and Helen watched me, waiting. I made some sort of answer like, What do you mean? But they shook their heads; we had a history to get to the bottom of, now.

Of course I'd always been jealous, she said, which was perfectly natural, given that she'd taken the man I first loved. But didn't I understand how I'd won out in this situation? How lucky I'd been, and how her girls had suffered? Could I possibly imagine how hard it had been for her girls to lose their father? How deeply my relationship with him had damaged them?

In the dark I saw my father stroke his beard and nod.

It went from there, as the light faded and the city began glittering. It slid into a dark, mirrored labyrinth, during which two more bottles of prosecco were popped, a labyrinth in which a monster was needed, a monster that might well lurk behind any troubles with fathers and men I'd spilled at the table but—far more importantly—surely lurked behind Jenny's. Helen said that of course she had needed to get her girls away from him. And once we'd stepped to the edge of the split, we slid in deep, into my mother, and I was told such intimate details that it was like being pressed into her body, and again what she'd done on the bloody ship, until at some point something slipped in the dark and the blurring lights of the city and all the mirrors along the way and I *became* her, my father with his sixth glass of bomb lost track.

All you do is fuck and fuck and fuck, he said. You are nothing but—.

Helen rose quickly and said, I'm sorry, Jane. That's it. He's gone. You'd better go to bed.

I ran down the marble stairs and locked the door and stood staring at the dark mirror, clutching elbows, teeth jammed, as if I'd explode from the compaction, Anthony and

Paul and Daddy, my mother and me, Helen the other woman, Jenny and me, all pressed together for twenty-five years, and I couldn't stand another second in that skin, that house, that metamorphic family. But I couldn't leave the Residence because Ahmed had locked the security gates, and I couldn't even call Maggy, because to dial long distance you needed a key.

The next morning, no trace. The ivied garden peaceful, the city humming in the distance, coffee poured from a silver pot into cups with the gold Australian seal.

When I think of that scene in the tower again, I feel the floral couch, the prosecco bubbling in my throat, and I try to hear what was said as clearly as possible. I can look through the darkness of that night and see a mother struggling with the dissolution of her daughter, a mother perhaps craving absolution, and a man still confirming the cause for his actions, a man who'd hoped that this enterprise would turn out all right—a pair of people so desperate in the water that they must push down any head to stay up.

I can do this, and believe it, and feel empathy, if it's true. But I don't know if it is. And I don't know if it's right to excavate living people, try to dig out their secrets so that I can create an intelligible line. And I also don't know if it's honest to imagine that I can distance myself from this story: not still wonder why, for their story to hold, others must be pushed under.

———

In the Residence, partway down the hall to the master bedroom, was a gate. You wouldn't see it without knowing to look, it was embedded in the ceiling, but Helen had pointed it out once, glancing back over her shoulder and smiling as I followed her down the hall. The gate would drop if the place was attacked, she said; it would drop and protect the ambassador and his wife. Separate from anyone else in the house: the chef, laundrywoman, maids, butler, guests, maybe even any children on the wrong side. Like that secret place in the Fifth Avenue hallway where the garden trellis turned to bamboo.

That gate I also see like this: as the film that seemed to drop in my father's eyes when they shifted into protocol, the established story. The film that took all those family portraits, the film that said, No harm done! The film that seemed the crucial belief that the enterprise had not gone wrong.

A similar gate fell in Paul's eyes; maybe the device comes with being a diplomat. But Paul didn't seem so much to stand behind his gate as fiddle with it as he liked. He knew perfectly well that the gate was a story, and that back there on the other side was what was *really* going on. And he seemed to like being able to give a glimpse of the truth if he wanted, otherwise setting his face hard and not giving an inch.

I told my father that I did not want to call him *Daddy* anymore; the word felt childish. I wanted to call him something else, maybe *Father*. But he wouldn't have this; *Father* was already taken, he said. So I tried *Edward*, but he wouldn't have that, either, because only his wife and friends called him by name. (*Why do you want to use my first name?* he wrote. *After all, I'm not Paul!*) I decided I couldn't call him anything, which meant I could have no relation with him at all. Which, of course, wasn't true. There was no escaping, no getting out of that house.

I didn't see Jenny when I was there, but she sent a letter her mother wanted me to read, saying Jenny sent me her love.

"Don't you know how important you are to her?" Helen said, following me through that enormous living room with the letter in her hand. "I know you've never cared for her, but you're terribly important to Jenny. She loves you very much."

Helen said this to me often, and each time I felt compacted, wanted to break free and out. From that word *love* mostly, that ruined word *love,* and this impossible family.

I still don't like the word *love*; it makes me hostile. It demands an equal answer and so rarely seems true. Yet when it does seem earnest, what does it mean? An Anthony I knew when I was fourteen, the first one whose tongue touched mine, and then this other Anthony ten years later, both said too often, *I love you.* I told them the phrase seemed cheap and asked them to say it less. But what I learned with the second Anthony was that he loved me the way you might love *dulce de leche* ice cream, love having that sweet cold stuff in your mouth. A happy, consuming, acquisitive love. Which isn't worth much, because appetites shift.

My sister and her daughters say *I love you!* at the end of each phone call, and they mean it, just not necessarily when they say it. When they say it on the phone it's an amulet, hopeful, warding off hijacking or crash. *I love you! The last thing we said was we loved her, so she knows.*

Then there's the word *love* at the ends of those letters, my father's, Helen's, the girls' (*I love you and miss you!*). Here it seems a prescription, as if it might come to mean what it says or at any rate proves in writing that the intent was there. In Maisie's letters, the ones she'd sign *all my love — lovingly*, adding new words for love in the last sliver of space — the word is alive, reaching warm hands through water and wind. The next time the word meant as much was in the negative. *I'm not in love . . . so don't forget it . . .* Refusing to have anything to do with it, to admit that need at the core.

Albert parsed the word in one of his last letters, turning to dictionaries, showing his old schoolmaster heart.

> *With my love and affection (not really the same) to you.*
> *G.P.P. Albert XX*
>   *"love" = fondness, paternal benevolence*
>   *or "affection" = emotion, a more mental state or a*
> *more physical affair (so says "Concise Oxford Dictionary")*

Albert wrote with an old fountain pen and sprinkled his letters with poetry. His marriage did last a lifetime, fifty-six years, even as pretty, preening Maisie lost an eye, got a glass one, and then lost sight in the other eye, too; even as she became frail and broke her wrist; even as paranoia seized her and made her snappish. Still he wrote, until she died, *Noth-*

ing will separate us. An old fairy-tale couple, twining together as trees.

Theirs is a good story about love. At the end of his life, Albert wrote an account of their courtship in his old, watery hand. It's sentimental but suffused with a love he held his whole married life, love not choked at each breath with jealousy, indistinguishable from void.

But my father has stressed that he had not truly loved my mother. In a letter, and at lunch one day with many old friends, and in that tower, he said how miserable they had been. To rationalize, maybe, to show consistency. As if love weren't something that could come into being and then fall away, change its intensity or hues. Either there is love or there is not: no lingering fond memory; cut her out of the photo.

And I have told him I never loved him, either. *Not only do I not love you but I don't like you, I don't care about you at all.* Although, of course, just saying these words undid their meaning, just sitting locked with him at a table, clenching cold hands under the red-and-white checked cloth as my eyes and tongue blackened, unable to get up and leave him, yet unable not to say those words, and, above all, unable to get what I wanted, which was not to need to say those words because I knew he loved me and always had.

Oh, the word *love* makes me hostile. It's like a ripping burr I can't get out of my skin.

Jenny had said her clean words about Anthony, but he'd said something about her, too. He knew the family story. After dinner at the Residence that night, he had called me and said, "She just seems like a fucked-up little girl."

I'd written in the blue Reagan notebook in Canberra that our parents had finished with the story but that for us it was only beginning. This wasn't true: or it was for me, but not Jenny. I was still caught in the family nets like a baffled moth, but she'd slipped out of them and flown on, into tighter ones. When she'd gone back to Sydney, apparently she was met by that boyfriend who didn't like chairs, and he had the usual bad treats in his pocket, and she went under again.

10

Home economics, domestic arts. Dora had been trained in this, a real subject for a young Australian woman in 1920. How to keep milk and meat without refrigeration; how to arrange time, funds, water, and fuel in the heat and dryness of a small South Australian town, within the schedules of men who delivered produce, and the seasons, the different fruits each might bring or withhold—how to manage with care each substance that came into the house. There's a pleasure in keeping linens fresh and floors swept and not letting any fruit rot, wasting nothing. You see this in Dora's accounts of life then. Her house was small but thoroughly kept, every surface imbued with her hands, thrift, and thinking.

When I visited her on that trip to Australia, she was near eighty and woke early, washed and dressed and then sang in the kitchen, a singing that rose into trills of delight but stopped cold when she saw me. She was never warm like my mother, but not unkind, either: dry and contained. Her pleasure seemed to be in keeping her house as she liked, and having in it a loved visitor, but having that visitor in another room sleeping, not awake and marring the world she'd made.

She knew one of the great things to know: how to make your own home and be content in it, alone.

I'm like Dora this way: I feel a wave of joy when I'm in my kitchen and the place is ordered and I have the food I need, plentiful but not enough to be wasted. It's a feeling of modest contentment. But if things are missing or broken or dirty, unease agitates through the place into me, as if everything will split apart.

Homemaking: The term sounds trite and has ruffles. Yet it stands for an enormous act of will, whereby you leash the globe and make it revolve around the incidental spot you've put your bed and table and cups. You've *made* that place your center. When all the while the world is out there with uncontrollable rushing currents, reminding you you're nothing. So what an act of power to make your self home and sturdy.

Not that there isn't the opposite surge, which makes me want to walk toward my cats, put them in their carriers, take them to the vet, and say, We must do it now, I can't care for them anymore, and stand by the metal table watching as each one, watching me, stops breathing. Then to walk home and take each potted fan palm and bougainvillea and drop it out the fifth-floor window onto the sidewalk, or not even bother, not bother to water them once more or run my fingers over their fronds to smudge to death the spider mites, just leave the plants to die, why not. Then walk away from my books and files and bar-of-gold jewelry box with the ancient silver peacock and llama, and walk down the sixty-six stairs, away, leave my husband standing there stricken, and go somewhere else, go break up someone else's home, too.

Equal surges: Make things, break them. Make yourself, or break out.

A few years after the episode in Italy, Jenny apparently was pulling herself together again. She'd gotten rid of the boyfriend who didn't like chairs and now had a new one, a tall, older man who seemed good to her. In 1995 she flew to the United States to visit her aunts, uncles, cousins, half-brother, and father, and she made the telephone call she'd never made to me in Sydney. But I didn't hear the phone ring, and she left a message; she was already about to board the plane back to Australia, and again I missed her.

I was involved with Alex then, living with him in Philadelphia, in an old wrecked house we were trying to fix. Telephone wires hung from the kitchen ceiling, through which you could hear mice scraping. Between the kitchen and patio stood fogged glass doors that wouldn't slide; outside, a Tree of Heaven, strangled in ivy, wrenched up the patio bricks. Termite tracks rivered the kitchen walls in dry channels you could crack with your thumbnail, and on the living room's black-and-brown plastic tiles stood tea chests and stacks of Baedekers like badlands. For months I'd been on my knees screwing down sheets of plywood or on ladders scraping off wallpaper, sanding and sponging, slapping on mud after Alex hung sheetrock. Between my skin and the walls and floors was no difference, cracked mud and ochre paint sticking to my legs, sawdust thick in my hair. I was trying to work my way into the house, right into those walls and beneath those floorboards, not write or think but just hammer.

One day I stopped drilling and saw the light blink on the answering machine, and when I punched the button, there was Jenny. I stood in the wrecked kitchen, in the new empty quiet, her voice floating around me. I knew it but at first couldn't name whose it was. Then realized it was her, and the world swiveled. The kitchen and house were what I didn't recognize, some dislocated place, a house and another man I'd washed up with, both of which could dissolve again. Because her voice was the real thing, the constant thing, as if playing from inside.

On this visit Jenny gave me her last gift, through Paul. It's a Penguin writers' quotation book, something you pick up quick at the cash register at Borders. Unlike the books she'd given me earlier and marked with her florid signature and poems, in this one she wrote nothing. I keep opening it and looking for something I missed, a message, a quotation underlined or starred. But it's just a book she grabbed and bought and passed on, without wrapping. If her father hadn't told me, I'd never know it even came from Jenny.

By then I'd been writing for a few years. But Jenny had been writing since those poems she'd bent over in her big shirts in the dark, those scraps of paper she'd shoved into her impossible bag. She'd written ever since, but I'd never thought about it until she gave me this book. So this was another thing she and I shared, along with our fathers, brothers, names, birthdays, countries, pasts, and longings: everything but our blood.

———

After struggling with that house a few years, in 1998 Alex and I sold it and moved to Germany. Before leaving, we went to Rehoboth with Maggy. Those last days in the United States felt like an end, a queasy end at the edge of a continent.

At the beach, we dumped our towels, and Maggy and I rented a big blue and yellow raft. We pushed ourselves up on it side by side, its cool, wet, taut fabric under our arms, our legs in the water kicking. She's taller and goes out deeper than I do, and she rolls her eyes when I get nervous so I pretended not to mind, and together we kicked out far. The green waves rolled in slowly, and when we saw a good swell coming, we lurched around, kicked, caught it, and rode it in, screaming and tumbling into the froth, grating our legs on the sand. We got up and turned around and shoved back out.

But while we were out there in the rising, lowering water, something happened: A current began gently to tug at my legs. Not at hers, though, maybe because she was bigger, more balanced. I clutched the edge of the raft tightly, but the current kept pulling and my hands slipped from the edge, and with nothing to grip in the middle of the raft, I slid back until I'd fallen into the water and was gripping the plump edge on which my hips had just rested. Maggy didn't notice because we were still pushing out, rising over swells. But then the current pulled me away from the raft, and I held only the white cord. Then that slipped away, too, and so did Maggy; she and the raft floated free over a swell, while I was pulled the other way, toward the jetty of black rocks. She looked back over her shoulder and called, but I kept being pulled farther. When I tried to stand, I went under. I tried not to panic, but if I did what you're supposed to, swim with the riptide, I'd be thrown into the rocks. As I was about to crash into them and lifeguards splashed into the water, I finally got a foothold. I staggered out of the water and Maggy came, too, laughing, uneasy, and we went up to the dry sand.

Huddled in a towel, I didn't want to tell her that it felt like more was slipping away, something was ending.

That night we drove down the coast, along that road between dunes and bay where Paul and I once flew in his Mercedes, leaving Jenny behind on the grass. At his beach house, with him and his wife and Tommy, we sat around the picnic table, ate grilled fish and bean salad, drank wine, took pictures.

Paul looked pleased and kept saying, "This must be the first time we've all been together in, what, it must be twenty years." As if it were a real reunion, and Maggy and I were really his daughters, and we were a family.

Later Paul and his wife sent me a photo taken that night, set in a green bamboo frame. It's the picture that comes closest to those glossy photos of my father's family in a tropical garden. I sit on one side of the table beside Paul, just him and me, and I have the bright tense smile I always have beside him, and look the way I always feel then, glassy, privileged, uneasy, as if this position is both my right and my crime. Even as the photo is snapped, I'm imagining his real girls seeing this picture when they next cross the Pacific to visit him, because he still did not fly to them; I imagine them seeing this framed picture in his office downtown. Paul had displayed my books there, the first books I wrote, when I still used his name, and I can see him take each book out of his briefcase, regard the cover and shiny gloss of our name, place the book on a spot on the shelf, adjust it, then regard it with satisfaction. In his office evidently one saw no trace of his daughters. When Patricia came to visit once and saw my books on his shelves but no sign of herself or her sister, I am told, her shouting could be heard down the hall.

Maybe Patricia saw this picture of her father and me sitting side by side, but Jenny didn't. As we sat on Paul's porch that steamy night and he smiled like a father flush in the wealth of his children, looking satisfied that the damned thing had turned out all right, in Sydney his real daughter was about to buy heroin, although she'd been off it for years.

A few days after Rehoboth: Germany. The sky was heavy and gray, and after sleeping awhile I went out for groceries. Then climbed the sixty-six stairs to our apartment, dumped the Karstadt bags on the floor, and pushed the button on the blinking answering machine.

"Hi, Jane, it's Paul," her father's voice said. "Bad news. Jenny's dead."

I sat down. Just sat there, in an empty apartment on the fifth floor of a bare, new building in a small city in Germany.

My first thought was, I'm free.

My second was, But now it's too late.

Because I'd thought, I'd quietly counted on, Jenny and me seeing each other one day, or Jenny reading something I wrote, and her knowing that she was in me, too, that I knew what I'd done to her, what we'd done to each other, and that I was unutterably sorry.

———

251

She had gone through rapid detox but then apparently stopped taking the antidepressants she'd need to endure this, and sank, and by then even the little heroin she injected was too much. It was a month before her thirty-eighth, my thirty-seventh, birthday; depending on the time zones, on her boyfriend's birthday or Paul's.

Earlier I'd written a novel based on her, on us, one of the ways I first tried writing out this family. I'd thought of killing her at the end, but didn't. The novel begins with a scene in which the girl like her and the one like me are swimming, and one is terrified of going deep, and the other taunts her to make her swim out far. Then suddenly she — Debby — begins to struggle way off in the water, and whether she's drowning or a shark's got her the other girl — Alice — can't tell, and stands paralyzed, chest deep. She pictures Debby dead but realizes that if she dies she will have won, she will have become singular and loved at last. So Alice swims out to save her, and the girls struggle, clawing at each other to stay up. In the novel I would not let Debby die; I had her doing her best. She lives in a halfway house near Sydney and comes out one day to the cliff along which Jenny and I once walked. She climbs down the grassy path to the beach and stands ankle-deep in the water, in the wind, gazing across the Pacific, longing herself to America, to Washington, to a cold apartment with a thick white carpet, downtown. That's where Jenny stayed in my mind, on the beach by the cliffs of Sydney, longing.

After Paul's message, there were calls over the oceans with Maggy, my mother, Daddy, Paul. Paul's voice sounded like metal plunged into cold water and shocked even harder. What we talked about was flights; he was arranging his to Sydney and said he'd have his agent help me with one, too.

But then, in another call, my father asked me please not to come, said truly it would be better if only Maggy were there.

"Think of Patricia," he said, and his voice sounded wretched, and I could tell how awful this must be for him to say. "Just think if it was your own sister who'd died, how you'd feel. Hmm? It would be easier for everyone if you didn't come. You understand, don't you? With Paul there."

So I helped pay for Maggy's ticket and sent a lot of white roses. While everyone was in Sydney burying Jenny, I wanted to be where I could picture her, and Alex and I drove to Normandy, to the high grassy cliffs at Etretat. On the day of her funeral we walked on a cliff, on the windy grass. The day was overcast and breezy, the Channel gray, and on the cliff you could see how the jagged edge of the land stood in sloshing Atlantic water, you could picture the continents just splitting apart.

Maggy and Helen sent me photos later: the church service, men carrying Jenny's coffin drenched in flowers, the burial. It's a sunny day, high on a green cliff of Sydney, looking out at the Pacific. The light is brilliant, the sea blue and hazy. Her father, my stepfather, stands in the foreground of one picture, in a dark suit in the antipodean light, near the grave. He's not looking at the coffin or the hole in the sand, though; someone must have called his name, so he's turned to look back at the camera. His face is stern and ruined. Before him, a heap of white sand and an incredible number of flowers. Jenny loved flowers; I didn't know. But there are heaps of flowers, lilies and gerberas, the same flowers I'd had at my wedding on the Atlantic, a wedding her father attended, a wedding at which he strode over to me smiling and said, You look the way Marilyn Monroe *wished* she did. The same gerberas here on Jenny's coffin: yellow, white, coral, and red.

It's the sort of picture you can look at and look at but still not see what you want. The waves don't break, the clouds don't drift across the sky, and Paul does not turn his head again, he does not turn and face that hole in the sand, he just looks back toward me. Although, of course, he does not look at me. I'm not there; I've been asked not to come. But that is how it will always feel. And the picture never shifts to the right, the lens never slides over enough to show Jenny. She lies unseen in her coffin, in the shadow that falls by the white heap of sand, beneath all the gerberas, which are all facing up, all facing the sun and us still living, not her.

After the funeral, after the reception, back at the apartment, Paul called me. He picked up the phone with everyone around, Patricia standing across the room; he must have put on his glasses and taken out his little phone book and then dialed the numbers to reach me in Germany.

Well, Jane, it's all over, he said.

He might have said another word or two, but all I could hear then was Patricia screaming: *Even now, even now, I can't believe you're calling her!*

Looks like I better go, he said, and hung up.

I put down the receiver, turned back to the gray silence of Karlsruhe.

But in Sydney, Maggy told me, even she couldn't stand it. She walked out, rode the elevator downstairs with her swimsuit, dropped into the pool, and sank to the bottom, the quiet.

It is an old graveyard, where Jenny is buried. Or as old as such a graveyard can be in Australia, that huge island with no British bones in the soil when Captain Cook first stepped upon it. Even the bones of my grandparents don't lie there: Dora, Herbert, Maisie, and Albert are ashes in boxes in drawers. Jenny's bones lie in the soil of a cliff you see rising crimson from the Pacific as you fly in on Qantas, a cliff Cook saw, swarming with birds. Around Jenny's grave are others, the remains of the first settlers and their children, the ones who didn't survive this strange new world. Inscribed on the gravestone of a little girl laid to face the ocean: *What hopes have perished with you, our daughter.*

After Jenny died, I tried again to put her in a novel and this time made her a ghost, a dead twin. A needle apparently was the last thing she touched before falling to her kitchen floor. At the time I was also using needles but, of course, for an opposite reason: I was trying to get pregnant, jabbing needles full of hormones into my stomach each morning. But it turned out that again we were both opposite and the same: Jenny had been trying to have a baby, too. She, like me, was failing. And I imagine this was one failure she just could not bear.

Because then you really are closed, and finite, and won't slip out of your skin. Like living and being finished at once.

There is no causal connection between the last thing Jenny and I shared and the story of our family. But I can't shake the feeling that there is, that a black hole had run through each of us ever since we'd been pulled from that bathwater long ago and gone our separate ways, and that she finally fell into hers.

After Jenny died, my mother sent a card for my birthday with a check to help pay for Maggy's ticket to Sydney, because, she wrote, *What happened to poor Jenny was my responsibility, too, way back.* My father sent a check, too, and wrote, *Happy birthday, but I won't say many happy returns of this particular one because there'll be too much pain in it for all of us.* Helen wrote, *We will be remembering you too on the 29th.* The night of our birthday I sat in the glass wintergarden in the dark, with a candle and a bottle of red wine and a white rose I'd bought to be Jenny. I wrote to her, words I couldn't even read between the darkness and wine and crying. Then burned the letter so the smoke words would have some obscure chance of reaching her, and burned the rose as well.

On our birthday my father's local paper printed an article he wrote about the "war on drugs" that had failed to save his child. He cites everything Jenny had tried for a decade: detox, psychotherapy, methadone, acupuncture "to help compensate for genetic deficiencies in the brain's natural chemistry; deficiencies lying behind the chronic relapsing brain disease from which addicted people suffer . . . Fallen addicts are not weak. They were wounded and disarmed from the outset."

Later Helen wrote to me about Jenny's slide into addiction and said how sorry she was I had never known the real Jenny except when we were young. *And often those encounters were filled with a certain amount of pain due to the rivalry for the two fathers. Although there is always pain when a child . . . it is regrettable beyond saying that you four girls experienced so much of it due to decisions we made when you were all so young. I know that the four of us feel this very deeply.*

Paul has told me about "the big black guy" who lived in his building near Dupont Circle, and he's speculated that it was this man who got Jenny hooked. He mentions this big black guy and leans back on his sofa with a scotch and squints, as if replaying those days, trying to pick one, to find the beginning of the ruin of his daughter. Helen said that Jenny's problem began with amphetamines during exams in college. I remember a night at the beach on Cape Cod, when we four girls went to a bonfire and drank beer for maybe the first time. Maggy and Patricia drank more than Jenny and I, so when we got home and found Daddy and Helen up waiting, those two rushed upstairs while Jenny and I strode forward, blithe and brash and glowing. Of course they smelled it. And the next day gave us a talking-to: We might think we were just sipping beers now, said Helen, but beer led to marijuana, and marijuana led to heroin. I stared at her in terror, but at the same time heard a little voice say, *She's crazy.* Yet she would probably say that what she saw in the bonfire came true. Beer by the bonfire and that big black man: things that could carry you off.

I try to imagine that lustful moment on the edge, that moment when you could dive in, go under, lose consciousness.

Or you could not; you could turn from that alluring blackness and step back into the ordinary world with its ticking
clocks and the body you'll be trapped in until you die. And
even if it's a fine body, healthy and lovely and lithe and smart,
still it's *you*, and for that you hate it, you hate the mind that
circles inside like a rat. You can just plunge out and be gone
from yourself. That's what I imagine Jenny wanted. I know
that's what I've wanted, when I've done what I've done.

Jenny had climbed deep into caves, she'd owned a car for
a day before crashing it, she'd gone diving so she could swim
near sharks. That day in Sydney, thirteen years before she
died, as we stood on a cliff and gazed at the Pacific, she told
me about diving. She told me that off the coast of New South
Wales she'd swum out to the nets that are placed there to
keep sharks away. She told me that she saw plenty of sharks
caught in the nets down there, dead sharks, eyes empty, long
gray bodies swaying cold in the dark.

"But *listen*, Jane," she said. "The thing *is*—" and this was
the point of her story, the part she'd been waiting to tell, like
her father, loving the jolt of terror "—the thing *is*, Jane, the
sharks I saw weren't trapped coming in. They'd been trapped
as they tried to swim out."

Jenny probably never found an answer to the question she asked that night in New York. I've never found it. There isn't one, just the stories our four parents might tell or the glimpses they'd give, stories that are each true enough. And if we had learned a single true story, would it have made a difference? The answer didn't matter; the question should never have mattered so much.

I've thought about asking my four parents what happened in 1965. They will not welcome this book, and I could not ask for their stories without saying why, and I think this would only make their stories more stiff, more formal: a filtering gate, held up against me. But there's no point speculating how they would fashion their stories, as I can't ask. It would be stealing, asking to have something not mine, whereas what I remember and think is my own.

The subject almost, but not quite, came up recently with my father. I was driving with him and Maggy's little girl, Cate, along a hilly road among weird geological formations and outlet stores in an industrial part of Italy, where my father had bought a farmhouse upon retiring. Somewhere among these eruptions of stone was supposed to be a stripe of the fabled mineral released by a comet that had extinguished the dinosaurs, and I was leaning out the window trying to see it in the jagged stones. Cate was carsick in the back seat, as truck fumes swirled in and we swung around curves and rattled over hills, so after a while we put her in the front seat to keep her from throwing up, and I climbed into the back. As she moaned and shut her eyes and pressed her hands to her forehead, I talked to distract her and hit on the topic of childhood injuries. That got her attention.

What was the worst thing that had ever happened to her? Broken finger? Black eye? Really bad cut?

She sat up and began bouncing in her seat, telling stories about dog bites and fingers jammed in doors. Then I told her about when Maggy was six and I was three, and one evening we were running around wild in slippery new Mary Janes, and Maggy skidded and hit her head on the corner of a stair. She screamed, there was blood all over the floor, she got a butterfly bandage. Cate knew this story and liked hearing it again, legend, twisting around and gazing back at me with her big opal eyes.

My father glanced up in the rearview mirror. "I don't remember that," he said. "Quite sure?"

Yes, I was sure. He squinted to remember, shook his head. "But I just don't recall it. In Washington?"

Yes, I said. In 1965.

Surely he'd recall it, he said, if it had happened. Surely

I was much too young then to remember anything. I must have gotten it wrong or made it up. But I had the staircase and banister right, and how slippery the floor was beneath our new shoes, and the butterfly bandage Maggy wore on her forehead, and Cate nodded violently to affirm the scar, so finally he admitted he just couldn't recall; perhaps he'd been out that evening. He glanced at me again, though, looking troubled, and his eyes went back to the hot winding road.

We were on our way to swim at the house of a friend of his, another Australian who'd landed in Italy. The topic that afternoon got to cigarettes and how much everyone missed the little elegances of smoke, and I described my father's orange cigarette drawings in the dark when I was four. Again he squinted at me, straining to see what I meant.

"But I just don't remember ever coming in with a cigarette!" he cried. And why should he, why would anyone, it would be like remembering brushing your teeth. But as I got up to swim, I suddenly wondered, and maybe he did, too: Had it even been him? Or was it not my father but Paul who'd drawn those glowing pictures in the dark all those years ago?

As we drove home, he caught my eye again in the rearview mirror, smiled quickly, and said, "So do you remember much else from Australia then?" He seemed good humored, just curious, but there was something in his voice and eyes — something that seemed concerned with collecting whatever he'd left behind inadvertently and would like safely back in his pocket.

"Hmm?" he said. "Remember much else from those days?"

I shrugged. "Sure," I said, but didn't go on, partly because I liked seeing him troubled, but partly because it would be too much, make me too weak, to reveal all I'd hoarded. The rock where I'd wait for him to come home, or the mark on my foot in the shape of Australia I've always believed I got when I tripped on a stone, running home when he called me to dinner.

His glance darted once or twice between the road and me, but he and I are both mulish enough that after just one more hopeful "Hmm?" he didn't ask again. And I wondered what images might still be burning in the darkness behind his eyes, what, after forty years, still flashed inside him, let out on his blackout nights, the black itself streaming like light.

Because my mother is the one I know best, I've heard more of her story than the others', and I've worried that this isn't fair, that I must learn their versions, too. But then I think, No. They've had forty years to speak up. In fact my mother hasn't told much at all, as if it were a dream, and she still can scarcely believe that it happened. She does have a few fixed memories and has told me these in such a way that I've absorbed them and know that no matter how I try to see through them, they've colored my vision. She says, "Oh, the others did it first." She crosses her arms and is certain. But she doesn't seem really to *know* it, to have proof; she only believes it, just as I wanted to believe the opposite. Because I'm closest to her, I try hardest to look into the gaps of what she says to find a darker version of her, one closer to how she might have been seen by the others.

She has embedded in her mind the phrases that signaled the end of her marriages: Helen's overheard, *There's a man at this party, and his name is Edward Cummins, and he's mine, so hands off.* Six years later in South America, the ambassador telling her, *Higamous, hogamous, woman's monogamous. Hogamous, higamous, man is polygamous.* I picture her hearing these words amid music and clamor, leggy and glamorous and a little drunk, and upon hearing them become that much more abandoned, fling out a hand, let an internal door fly open so that she could do whatever the bloody hell she wanted because *they* were, after all. Each time she's recounted these moments, though — thirty and forty years since the events — there's been a pause when she gazes away into the trees, the night sky, and in her face are hurt and bewilderment.

She's said many times that she and my father really did love each other, that it wasn't all bad. The nastiest thing she ever told me was something ugly my father apparently said one of those dark nights in the little Canberra house. This was in the kitchen where she vamped for Paul in her yellow swimsuit. Yet the interesting part of this detail isn't the ugliness of what she says my father said but what she revealed of herself in telling it: She stressed the *littleness* of the house in Canberra, its littleness having disappointed her, the Stuarts' house being far more grand. This was a new angle on the story. It altered the equation I'd worked out, that Helen had gone toward the safer man, and the one more likely to succeed. Another item to file with this: My mother had met

Paul, with my father, in Washington, before even returning to Canberra.

The hardest thing she told me is this: My father said either she must file for divorce or he would, because he wanted that woman. There it all is in that raw verb *want*: to be wanted, or not to be wanted, the only measure of value. Just *being* is not enough — and not even an option, because you can't isolate yourself from the wretched human economics of desire and desirability, the currents of value and valuation that forever stream between bodies and eyes. Lucretius, like Epicurus, said: Eliminate your wants, and you will eliminate the pain of not getting. Epicureanism is not about pleasure but about avoiding pain. Want nothing, and you will not suffer; plug up the leaky jar. But you cannot plug up the jar and still live. You have no choice but to be porous and leak, to want and love, and need to be wanted and loved, and I have to keep learning this again and again, and it is painful every time.

The last thing she has told me: One night when we were all at the Stuarts', she'd been giving Jenny and me our bath. She stood from sudsing us in the water, stepped to the door, and saw, in the dimness of the next room, my father and Helen embrace.

Paul has told me nothing about those days. He'll make a remark like, Helen's whole family is crazy. They're nuts! and break into that gunshot laugh. Perhaps something can be divined from these words, I don't know. He did tell my mother a few details, and she passed these on to me — so technically, I suppose, they belong to her account and not his.

He has said: In Peru, Helen walked into the sea one day and swam out. Straight out into the Pacific. I picture him standing on the shore, fists at hips, squinting, and damned if he knows what's the matter with her, tightening his heart against whatever he felt as her blond head, her young arms, slashed away from him into the sea.

And he has said to my mother: Of course the other two were at it first. At the beach, near Canberra, where both young families went for a weekend. He told my mother the others started then. For proof he cites that utterly ambiguous phrase they'd whispered: *Screw your courage to the sticking point.*

He has said nothing else. He has let nothing slip. Because he's not like my father, never alters no matter how much scotch he's drunk, never misses a curve.

There are some cracks in him, though. On one of his visits to Germany, Alex and I drove him through Alsace. It was a bright day, and Paul sat in the passenger seat, I sat in the back, the car speeding smoothly along the ribboning road, the wind whipping past; it could have been Australia again. I mentioned something about my Aunt Joan, my mother's sister, whom Alex and I had just run into by chance in a train station.

I'm trying to remember, Paul said, which one of your mother's sisters that is. She's got so many goddamned sisters. I remember Marilyn and some of the others, but I just can't remember which one is Joan. And they're all crazy, he said, turning to me with that collusive smile.

I made some joke to cover his mistake. Because Marilyn

is not my mother's sister, but Helen's. He'd forgotten which of the two women I belonged to.

About Helen he has said: Now *there's* a woman who's never lost her looks. And: She was always a terrific cook, just terrific. There's not much to go on, but from the little there is, I see a man who lost a woman he did not want to lose. His marriage with my mother, I think, passed in a blur.

He is a man who has fed and petted a neighborhood cat for years, his eyes as he strokes this tattered animal the same tender soft eyes as when he once held my hand. On one of his last visits to Germany, we climbed the spiraling dark steps of an old fortress tower, inside, dark and cold. I had gone first and, as I came to the light at the top, I looked back over my shoulder; in the shadows behind me, Paul climbed the steps on hands and knees. I looked away fast. But a moment later, when he strode into the light, he was tall again, Paul, and regarded the city and the Black Forest, all stretched out before him.

Helen has said little to me, either. Just: Don't you see? I had to get my girls away from their father.

I romanticize Paul, as my mother said, and one of my favorite fabrications is this: He was CIA, not regular Foreign Service, and brought down a South American government or two. Helen hadn't known this when she married him, but perhaps she found out in Peru. Frightened and angry, maybe she threw her towel on the shore and ran into the water, began to swim out . . . But finally stopped, gasping, regained her breath, treaded water, thought for a time, and swam in.

And soon, in Canberra, she met a more suitable man. Not only suitable but unhappy.

This is pure fantasy. But it suits me and seems to work.

Of course she had to get her girls away from their father if she thought he was dangerous. But what I have wondered is this: Did she tell my father that, and did he believe her? Did he knowingly let his own girls go with a man he believed to be dangerous? And my mother: What did she think?

But was that man truly dangerous? Were both? Or was neither? Was neither worth any of this at all?

My mother's story and my father's, Helen's story and Paul's, have moved ever farther apart over the decades, like specimens of a single plant transported by splitting, drifting continents, slowly evolving different stems and leaves. One thing I know is that however the split happened, it had to. Those four did what they needed to do, as I would do now myself. Who wouldn't shake off a shadow if he could? Trade in a trapping life for a new one? Especially if it seemed that everything was even, that no one would be hurt.

Now and then I decide to love my father easily, to push my way through all the asphyxiating clutter. It's a relief, it's like that gate in the Residence hallway sliding open, and I can just flow through it and love him. But when he actually stands before me, I can't do it. The gate slams shut inside me, and I can't afford to love him or tell him or give him a thing.

———

A friend of Nicholas's once said, when I was visiting my father, "You haven't any idea what it was like before you arrived. They don't put out the special silverware and plates for Nick and the others. That's all just for you."

I'd seen only the presentation, impressing and dazzling and making me think blackly of our chipped plates at home. But now, another glimpse through the mirror: Maybe before all those visits, my father had moved through the apartment or Residence making sure the dishes were turned to show the gold Australian seal, fresh lilies stood in vases, silk pillows were plumped. Maybe he had moved about humming. But maybe Helen had been the one to do most plumping and arranging, and maybe the girls had been told to clean their rooms, clean up their acts, for Daddy's real daughters. And maybe once the place was readied and Maggy and I walked in, so much bitterness burned in the air that my father would have to tamp his pleasure, having shown such favoritism before we'd even arrived.

I've seen this man sometimes. Fussy and jolly as we cook dinner, he waves me from the cutting board, he throws up his hands in despair at how I chop garlic or spin the greens, he shakes rivers of salt into the pasta water and brushes my worries away with mock impatience — but all he wants, maybe, is to show how well he can make lemon pasta; maybe what he wants amid all the teasing and mocking is to please me.

My father has praised my books and said that he's proud of me. I like the praise. But when he says he's proud, when he says this now, I can't help it: I grow bitter that he thinks he has a right to be proud. He wants, now, to help me buy a house, as he's helped the others. But it's too late: I can't let him own anything about me. I don't know what he can now do. I cannot be pleased.

When we're apart it's easier, and we are apart all but three or four days a year. We send each other a card or message every few months, short, simple things that try. I send him a drawing I think he'll like; he sends me postcards of paintings or places he knows I like. The Tomb of the Diver, Friedrich's dark moons, palm trees far north in Scotland.

In the past few years he's acquired a tic: Each time we've spoken on the phone—perhaps once a year—and are about to sign off, or each time we've visited and are about to part, he says, "Love you lots!" I don't know what to do when he says this. It's not *I love you;* it's not a phrase that demands I say anything back. So I don't. Or I'll say, "Give my love to Helen!" or something that seems suitable without going too far, without actually saying *I love you, too.* It's like writing *Love* at the end of a letter, a formality that doesn't mean much; there isn't even a pronoun, a subject.

But the phrase does mean something. Surely he is saying something. And he is doing it just as you do in a letter, that gesture that tries to hold on as you're about to fall away into the huge world again. *With all my love! Lovingly! . . . Give my kind love to Papa.* The moment itself is always awkward: I make my inadequate answer and hang up or get in a car and drive off, or he's the one to drive off. And it's then that the ripping starts again, that he's leaving all over again, disappearing invisible into the world once more, and once again I do not have him.

Sometimes I think that now Jenny is gone the tragedy is played out. We are all worn out with this impossible story, with the volumes of words we have never been able to say to each other; we just try to get along. We meet most years for two or three days, go together to museums or restaurants, talk about presidential races, or books, or Richard Serra's serpentine sculptures, and there's real pleasure in all this. We laugh, even, we grow giddy. If only we could just be these people talking and caring just enough about each other, just *be* the people we presently *are*, freed of those ancient nets. But those nets are always there, tangled in our ribs or throats, visible in our eyes each time we remember.

In Germany recently, when my father and Helen visited, I complained of a scratch in my eye; it wasn't much, but the eye grew red and watered, so Helen came over to look. We stood in my apartment, by a large mirror, near a revolving bookcase full of Ovid and Aeschylus, the light green and watery on a rainy German day. She held my chin and tilted my face to see. I both looked at her and tried to look away, tried just to show the hurt eye. Whatever was wrong I don't remember; it was soon gone. What I remember is Helen touching my chin, her eyes looking carefully at mine. I might have held my breath. Then she leaned back, but didn't step away, and with my chin in her hand kept looking into my eyes. Differently now: quizzical, absorbed.

My god, she murmured after a moment, your eyes are just beautiful! She seemed surprised, as if she'd never seen them before. She looked more closely. There's a deep blue ring around the iris, she said, and near the pupil there's dark ochre, or gold . . .

All I could think was: She's seeing me, she's seeing the substance that's actually me, no one else is in the way.

I didn't move, barely breathed. Across the room, gazing at us, my father did not move, either. His face seemed peaceful in the cool German light.

When I'm with Helen and meet people, they say, "Oh, you look just like your mother." She and I smile and declare that we're flattered and don't bother to make the correction.

When I'm with my mother and meet people, they say, "Oh, you look *just* like your mother!" And we both smile and say that we're flattered.

My mother and Helen don't look too much alike, yet it's true I look like both of them. I sometimes imagine that the blood of both women runs in me, as if they were my true and only parents, and it's from the two of them, their strengths and secrets and beauties and failings, that I've been constructed. And often I think, despite all the darkness, what an odd gift to have had two of everything. A sparkling, black, precious possession.

When I look down at my feet and calves, in nice thonged sandals and with my toenails polished, I see Helen. I especially see her in my calves and feet when I do what I have often done, living in Europe: walk around ruins or galleries, looking. I feel like a lady then, a new Madame Merle, pausing before a painting, pressing a finger to the guidebook.

When I look at my arms and hands, I see my mother. Stretch out my fingers: There she is. Strong arms, lean, with gold hairs and sunspots, nails blunt. Hands for doing things, cleaning, tearing up a plant. When I get up at six, make coffee, assemble my papers to teach — then quickly water a dry philodendron before running out to catch the bus — I see my mother.

When all four parents look at me, what they see sooner or later is the absence of Jenny. I look in the mirror and see it, too.

A friend asked me the other day, "Do you ever feel like your own self?" We were in a loud dining hall having lunch, and the question seemed so indulgent I laughed. An hour later I stood in a bathroom stall staring at a message about personal hygiene, and didn't know how to pull myself together, and had to go out soon and teach.

But of course I pulled myself together and went out. Because Jenny was the one ruined, not me.

Lucretius is the ancient philosopher I've always liked most. He sees atoms streaming in straight lines, elementary particles that, endlessly falling, would never bump, never clump or congeal and begin to form objects, but would stream eternal and lifeless in parallel lines. There must be an initial slip, a stir, something that makes one atom swerve into another and send it spinning and crashing, so that the lines become marvelously tangled and life begins. You need entanglements.

All the entanglements in this family: the original split, that southern cross; Jenny and me with our toes clenched in the bath; Jenny and me in our twin beds with her words splitting open the darkness; Paul forgetting whose daughter I am; my father looking at me but seeing my mother. All of this formed the tissues that made us.

Yet when I say this sort of thing to Maggy, she seems baffled, she shrugs. She escaped all of it and made herself otherwise. And so simply. The other day she said, "I just pretended Daddy was a nice uncle." That was it. She didn't fix her soul to him, didn't need a father to shine light through her, to make her visible and live.

Whatever made those four do what they did I will never know. I can keep puzzling over the stories, sliding the pieces around until maybe one day they'll lock into place. What I can also do is walk away. Just get up and leave that puzzle behind, go outside into the brilliant light, because Miami Beach is where I live now, alone, and look into the green water at clear, needle-nosed fish, watch an iguana suddenly run across my path, splash into the water, and swim off.

Recently I saw my friend William and asked him about those nights at Café Lautrec, when Jenny and he charged off to after-hours clubs. He told me a few details about the coke and the girls kissing in corners, but otherwise was confused.

"Jenny didn't work at Lautrec," he said. "You mean Amy."

Amy was someone else we knew in those days, also difficult and wild.

"Of course she did," I said. "Remember? You'd go there after work, and at first you didn't know she was my stepsister. And then I found out and thought it was funny, and we'd go there together. Remember? That's how you went to the after-hours clubs. You couldn't have known her or gone to them otherwise."

Still William was confused; he seemed sorrowful. Finally he shook his head. "I'm sorry," he said. "I just don't remember Jenny there."

I went to Café Lautrec to find someone who might have known Jenny, maybe a manager or the owner—she'd told me, with that gaze into her private sphere, about the wife of the owner demanding she be fired. Lautrec is on Eighteenth Street in Adams Morgan, and as I walked down the street in the hot June sun I was glad to see from a distance the huge mural on the façade, the big man in a red scarf and black hat. But when I reached the building, the windows were boarded, the place empty.

So I walked farther down Eighteenth Street, past her father's old apartment, where she'd stood in his bathroom in a haze of hair spray and smoke, smiling at me and herself in the mirror, wild to go. Her father had moved years earlier to a big house in Upper Northwest, near Deal. I kept walking down to George Washington Hospital to see again where Jenny had once been, up in the psychiatric ward. I just wanted to see it, some vaporous trace of her. But when I got to Washington Circle, there was a huge hole in the ground, the building razed. I looked stupidly up into the hazy air to where the sixth floor might have been, and pictured her up there still, sauntering down the shining hallway, flicking her bandaged wrist and bracelet as she blew kisses to the lunatics. With nothing but sky it was easy to squint and see her forever wandering, up there in a cube of air.

I kept walking, down to the Museum of Natural History. In the great dim hall where the blue whale hung from the ceiling, Jenny had stretched up her hands, claiming that whale, longing to be something larger than her own longing self.

But in the museum now hung no blue whale. I looked in the ocean room and the mammal room, among all the milling, chattering children, but found no suspended whale. When I asked a woman at the information desk, she said, "Oh, no, that whale's been gone a very long time. It wasn't even accurate."

Jenny wandering up on the sixth floor in the air, transformed to light and shadow. Like one of Ovid's girls who'd been raped and humiliated and turned into a bear but then, as a grace, altered once more, now to a constellation. Helen has done something you can do these days: designated a star to be Jenny's.

Maybe making a self is like writing. You start with nothing inside skin, or an empty white page. Out of this you conjure one frail figure, one living strand after another. Most strands are feeble and give way at a tug. But slowly some grow stronger, not watery and smudged to nothing between the fingers, but firm. Bit by bit this goes on. With luck what's in you is content there, and by content I mean contained: The flesh itself and the consciousness infusing it are not alien to each other but mutually owned. No one part, a hand governed by despair, slices open a wrist with a knife; no one part, a denying brain, just flees, leaving a soft, staggering body among strangers at night.

Making a self can be like writing, and now I think writing can be like home: a space you make that you dwell in and roam through for hours every day, a space that's absolutely yours.

And now that Jenny's gone the story seems over, and I can finally write it out.

I think of Jenny in her grave in the cliff outside Sydney. Then I see the other narrow spaces she'd been, where she and I had been fixed together: my extra twin bed on Barnaby Street, where the springs sighed on our birthday night when she came home alone. Or her twin bed in the pink room on Fifth Avenue, where she raised a foot in the darkness and split the night with her question. And that bathtub in Canberra at the start of our lives, when we looked at each other over the suds and pressed each other's wet pink feet, while my mother stood in the doorway and turned to see my father embrace Jenny's mother, and our story began.

The other day I saw in a dream the seal of Australia, the emu and kangaroo. It lay on a stone floor, cast as a shadow or as colored light through stained glass. When I saw the image, tremulous on stone, I felt rise from nothing that compounded sense of my father and home — again, that obscure pain for the lost man and lost place those seven, nine years when that ache lodged in my ribs. It's odd to think of excavating yourself and finding inside the things that were lost. Odder still to be tugged by these things, although they live only inside you.

I suppose it's the same, this yearning for love and home, for a place where we dwell at the center. Sometimes I think that memory, pain, and love all arose from the same quiet pool in the body: longing.